DO YOUR OWN ADVERTISING

G000055304

DO YOUR OWN ADVERTISING

SECOND EDITION

ALASTAIR CROMPTON

BUSINESS BOOKS LIMITED

Copyright © Alastair Crompton 1986, 1991

The right of Alastair Crompton to be identified as the author of
this work has been asserted by him in accordance with the
Copyright, Designs and Patents Act, 1988.

First published in September 1986 by
The Gold Farthing Press
9 The Drive, Esher, Surrey KT10 8DQ

Reprinted under the Hutchinson Business imprint 1987 and 1988
This (second) edition published in 1991 by
Business Books Limited
An imprint of Random Century Group Ltd
20 Vauxhall Bridge Road, London SW1V 2SA

Random Century Australia Pty Ltd
20 Alfred Street, Milsons Point,
Sydney, NSW 2061, Australia

Random Century (NZ) Ltd
18 Poland Road, Glenfield,
Auckland 10, New Zealand

Random Century SA (Pty) Ltd
PO Box 337, Bergvlei 2012, South Africa

Printed and bound in Great Britain by
Mackays of Chatham PLC, Chatham, Kent

British Library Cataloguing in Publication Data

A catalogue record for this book is available
from the British Library.

ISBN 0–7126–4985–9

CONTENTS

ACKNOWLEDGEMENTS

I'd like to acknowledge the help I have received in designing, writing and producing this book, from the following people.

My wife, who as a mother of two, and with a wide range of other interests and demands on her time, learned to type to produce the manuscript. Previously she had no secretarial skills; now she is a proficient p.a.

Bob Bernard, who designed the dust jacket, produced the drawing for it, and laid out many of the inside pages. He put up with my foibles and subjugated his own (probably better) judgement to my requests.

Martin Borland of Spectron Artists, London, who helped me with much of the artwork and secured permission for me to use it, both from the artists themselves, and the companies who originally commissioned it.

Daz Valadares, a media expert and director of a specialist media company, who checked Chapter 2 of the book.

Teresa McVeigh of the New York advertising agency Doyle Dane Bernbach, who (although she has never met me in her life) has helped with both DO YOUR OWN ADVERTISING and a previous book of mine.

Adrian Stenton, who acted as editor, indexer, and was generally helpful over continuity, layout and my atrocious spelling.

All of them are living proof that when it comes to a work of this kind no one does it on his own.

ALASTAIR CROMPTON

HOW TO WIN FRIENDS AND INFLUENCE PEOPLE

"The Reader's Digest" devoted 10 pages to this volume because, in their words, "From Mr. Carnegie's extensive reservoir of experience has come the wealth of anecdote and common sense lessons in human relations in which HOW TO WIN FRIENDS AND INFLUENCE PEOPLE abounds.

DALE CARNEGIE

JOHN D. ROCKEFELLER, Sr. once said: "The ability to deal with people is as purchasable a commodity as sugar or coffee. And I will pay more for that ability than for any other under the sun."

Wouldn't you suppose every college would conduct practical courses to develop this highest-priced ability under the sun?" To our knowledge, none has.

How to develop that ability is the subject of Dale Carnegie's amazing new book

A few years ago Chicago University and the United Y.M.C.A. Schools made a survey to find out the prime interest of adults. The survey took two years, cost $25,000. It indicated that their first interest is health, and their second, how to understand and get along with *people*, how to make people like you, how to win others to your way of thinking.

Wouldn't you suppose that after the members of this survey committee had decided to *give* such a course, they could readily have found a practical textbook? They searched diligently, yet could find none suitable.

The book they were looking for was recently published and overnight became a best seller. 36,000 copies were sold in three days of last week alone. More than 500,000 copies have been sold to date. IT IS OUT SELLING ANY OTHER BOOK IN AMERICA TODAY!

A New Book—and the Man Behind It

It is called *How to Win Friends and Influence People* and is written by the one man who is perhaps better qualified to write it than anyone else.

Dale Carnegie is the man to whom the big men of business come for practical guidance on the subject of getting along with people, dealing with them successfully, winning others to their own way of thinking. During the last 25 years he has trained more than 17,000 business and professional men and women among them some of the most famous in the country.

When he conducts his course on Public Speaking and How to Influence People in the ballroom of the Hotel Commodore, or The Pennsylvania, or the Hotel Astor the second largest hall in New York the place is packed to capacity. Large organizations such as The New York Telephone Co., Westinghouse Electric and Manufacturing Company, and many others listed elsewhere on this page have had this training conducted by Mr. Carnegie in their own offices for their members and executives.

This new book, *How to Win Friends and Influence People*, grew and developed out of that vast laboratory of experience. As you can judge from the panel at the top of this advertisement it is as practical as 24 years of actual successful experience with the problems of thousands of people in all walks of life can make it.

Consider the Case of Michael O'Neil

Michael O'Neil lives in New York City. He first got a job as a mechanic, then as a chauffeur.

When he got married he needed more money. So he tried to sell automobile trucks. But he was a terrible flop. He suffered from an inferiority complex that was eating his heart out.

On his way to see any prospect, he broke out into a cold sweat. Then, before he could get up enough courage to open the door, he often had to walk up and down in front of an office half a dozen times.

When he finally got in, he would invariably find himself antagonizing, arguing. Then he would get kicked out never knowing quite why.

THIS IS A BIG BOOK OF THIRTY-SEVEN CHAPTERS; INCLUDING:

The Big Secret of Dealing with People
Six Ways to Make People Like You Instantly
An Easy Way to Become a Good Conversationalist
A Simple Way to Make a Good First Impression
How to Interest People
Twelve Ways to Win People to Your Way of Thinking
A Sure Way of Making Enemies—and How to Avoid It
The Safety Valve in Handling Complaints
How to Get Cooperation
A Formula That Will Work Wonders for You
The Movies Do It. Radio Does It. Why Don't You Do It?
Nine Ways to Change People Without Giving Offense or Arousing Resentment
How to Criticize—and Not Be Hated for It
How to Spur Men on to Success
Making People Glad to Do What You Want
Letters That Produced Miraculous Results
Seven Rules for Making Your Home Life Happier

He was such a failure he decided to go back to work in a machine shop. Then one day he received a letter inviting him to attend the opening session of a Dale Carnegie course.

"It may do you some good, Mike. God knows you need it!"

He didn't want to go he was afraid that he would be out of place that there would be a lot of college men. But his despairing wife made him, saying, "It may do you some good, Mike. God knows you need it."

He went to the meeting, and other meetings of the course. He lost his fear. He learned how to talk charmingly and convincingly, how to make people like him at once, how to win friends and influence others.

Today Michael O'Neil is a star salesman for one of the country's largest manufacturers of motor trucks. His income has mounted and skyrocketed. Last year at the Hotel Astor, he stood in front of 2500 people and told a rollicking story of his achievements. Few professional speakers could have equalled his confidence or his reception.

Michael O'Neil is a salesman but his problem was exactly the same as that of thousands in other fields the fundamental one of getting along with people. The way it was solved is just one example of what Dale Carnegie's help has meant to more than 17,000 people in all types of endeavor. What Dale Carnegie has done for them he can do for you. Look at the chapter headings. They indicate the amount of hard-hitting, priceless information Dale Carnegie's book contains. But the subject is so intensely important that we say, look at this book without obligation. Then decide whether or not you want to own it.

Large organizations such as:

Westinghouse Electric Manufacturing Co.	Brooklyn Chamber of Commerce
New York Telephone Co.	Philadelphia Chamber of Commerce
Bell Telephone Co. of Pennsylvania	Philadelphia Electric Co. Philadelphia Gas Works Co.
American Institute of Electrical Engineers, New York	Carrier Engineering Corporation
McGraw-Hill Publishing Company, New York	Philadelphia Association of Life Underwriters

have had this training conducted in their own offices for their members and executives.

This new book is a direct result of Dale Carnegie's experience, the only working manual of its kind ever written to help people solve their daily problems in human relationships.

SEND NO MONEY

Try Dealing THIS WAY With People—for Just FIVE Days!

This book has been published for only a short time. Yet it is now something any other book—fiction or non-fiction—in America! The presses are now running continuously to turn out 5,000 copies daily.

When you get your copy simply read it; there are no "exercises" to be practiced. Then try for five days Dale Carnegie's simple method of dealing with people. Judge for yourself, in your daily social or business life, how easily whatever you do, say, or write can win the friendship and the hearty cooperation of others—instead of arousing resentment, friction, and even a negative response or no action at all.

It is not necessary to send any money now. You may pay for "How to Win Friends and Influence People" when it is delivered—with the definite understanding that the price of only $1.96 will be refunded to you if you wish it. If this book does what we claim, it will mean more to you than ANY book you have ever read. If it doesn't we do not want you to keep it. Mail this coupon at once.

SIMON and SCHUSTER, Dept. C-638, 386 Fourth Ave. New York

Only $1.96

SIMON and SCHUSTER, Publishers
Dept. C-628, 386 Fourth Ave., N.Y.C.

Please send me *How to Win Friends and Influence People.* I will pay postman only $1.96 plus few cents postage charge. It is understood that I may read it for 5 days and return it for refund if I then feel that it does not in every way live up to the claims made for it.

Name ....

Address ....

City .... State ....

Check here if you prefer to enclose $1.96 plus 6c New York Sales Tax WITH this coupon, in that case WE will pay the postage charges. The same refund privilege applies of course.

NOTE: If resident of New York City add 6c for City Sales Tax.

This advertisement was written in December 1936 and in the next three years it sold a million books. It was re-run so many times it became an advertising landmark of the Thirties.

viii

CREATIVE? WHO ME?

Before we begin I'd like to speak to the reader who's never written a word of advertising copy in his life, and doesn't believe he ever will. Just take a look at this advertisement for Dale Carnegie's famous book. There are no clever plays on words. You couldn't say this was a pretty piece of selling. Or witty, shocking, or arty. Yet this ad pulled in cheques and postal orders like you wouldn't believe.

You don't need to be a creative whizz-kid to write this kind of material. You don't need to be a literary giant either, in fact a First in Greats could be a positive disadvantage. You don't need Roget's Thesaurus, a Dictionary of Quotations, or to emulate a TV commercial you remember and admire. You don't even need to be very original or entertaining.

This ad is simply an outstanding example of the *craft* of copywriting. If, when you start to carry out the disciplines this book sets down, you become stuck for ideas or what to say next, turn back and look at "How to Win Friends and Influence People". If your writing is as plain, simple and as easily expressed as this, rest assured, you're creating great advertising.

FOREWORD

THE BIG SELL

Can you do your own advertising? If you've ever tried penning a slogan for your company and filled a waste paper basket with clichéd ideas, you'll know it's not as easy as it looks. But the answer is, yes, you can. And without the skills of a giant ad-agency behind you. What you need is the knack and the knack can be taught: how else do you think baby ad-men learn?

What you need is a system

A system that helps the mind concentrate on the essentials and get things into the right perspective and order. Clear, simple ideas into the brain bring clear, persuasive advertising out. Contrariwise, garbage in, garbage out. We're talking here mostly about advertising in print. This book sets out the secrets of producing any or all of the following:

* Newspaper Advertisements

* Trade and Technical Press Advertising

* Magazine Advertisements

* Radio Commercials.

* Leaflets

* Recruitment Advertising

* Brochures

* Classified Advertising

* Handbills

* Sales Letters

* Posters

* Direct Mail-Shots

* Ads on Buses

* Letter-box Drops

What about cinema and TV?

Film is different. So is television. If you want to be seen on telly you'll need a director, producer, lighting cameraman, focus puller, continuity girl, clapper boy, *et al*. Not to mention the scriptwriter and the know-how to clear your script through the various advisory bodies that decide what can and can't be seen on TV. The time-segments you buy to advertise on the box cost an arm and a leg, excluding the many thousands of pounds you shell out to make the commercial in the first place. This book assumes you don't want to compete with the detergent giants, the car-making combines, the mighty budgets behind hi-fi equipment, frozen food, baked beans and the like. You're in business in a modest way, your advertising budget is modest and it's unlikely that any company making TV commercials will give you more than a pleasant chat and a terrifying glimpse into the kind of costs you'll incur.

Selling in print

But your product is good, you know there's a market out there, all you have to do is reach them, talk to them persuasively, convince them that they need what you've got and tell them to send you a cheque today. That bit is important, and you'd be surprised at the number of ads that tell you their story but forget to tell you what to do about it.

Make no mistake, starting off with a blank piece of paper and a silent typewriter can be daunting. Where do you begin? How do you attract attention? Will they look at your sales leaflet for a couple of seconds then file it in the basket below their office desk? If you get it wrong, you've spent a lot of time and money and the customer hasn't heard you. Get it right and you can shape the habits of a nation.

The heart of the matter

Believe it or not, there are rules about creating advertising. Rules about how to pinpoint the limited number of customers you want, in a paper that's read by millions. Rules about how to select and then put over *your big promise*. Rules about laying everything out so it attracts the eye, stimulates the mind, and all points in the direction of making a sale. I'm not saying your word processor could do it; obviously you'll need to be able to express yourself just a little. But that can be the fun of it, shaping your words to raise a smile but, at the same time, get the message home.

The simple truth is, advertising works, and we have some pretty good ideas why it works. Right now, you're in a company where every penny counts and if you set aside money for publicity you want it to earn you back a much greater sum. You want your sales effort to be fast, effective and keep on selling. Remember, *truth* sells, lies and puffs don't. *Great advertising is the truth well told.* If you're looking for a guide on how to tell it, you've come to the right place.

CHAPTER

1

ARE YOU READY TO
ADVERTISE?
SOME CAUTIONARY
TALES.

"Out of every 100 products launched in a year, only three or four can be expected to survive".
Marketing Week.

CHAPTER ONE

It helps to understand right at the start that advertising is a selling tool: it is not a miracle worker. You would be foolish to believe that if your product isn't selling now, the position will change dramatically if you advertise. It might never change at all and to embark on any kind of publicity without first being sure that the product or service you are offering is the kind that people want can, quite literally, be ruinous. Advertising can find you customers. It can make people aware that you have something to sell. It can spread your story into parts of the country you cannot otherwise reach. It can inform hundreds of thousands of potential customers. It is one of the quickest ways to expand a market for a product *which you know is good.*

Advertising can add value to a product. It can give the buyer psychological reasons to buy; in other words, provide him with a justification for spending his money. Advertising can create images, it can inform and persuade, it can even entertain. It can make you famous (and it can make you infamous). But it can't, and never could, *improve the product itself.* Even in the big agencies, where much research and in-depth interviewing is carried out, many more new products fail than succeed. Massive funds can be put behind ideas that seem good at the time. They die horribly, amid much hullabaloo, the sound of heads rolling and accountants sucking their teeth. However confident you are, *never spend advertising money on a chancey product.*

How to get the skids under you

Here follows a cautionary tale. There was once a company that made tyres, and they were good tyres that stopped you sliding all over the place when it rained and the roads were like greasy poles. And the boss of this company said to his people, "Let us advertise these good tyres and see if we can get drivers speeding to our door". Only it wasn't his door; it was the doors of all the garages, forecourts and accessory shops that sold tyres. And so the campaign went forth, on television no less, and the drivers began to speed. Alas, what did they find? The good tyre-maker had not been able to get his tyres *distributed* in enough places, over enough of the country. So the drivers thought, "We're here now and we need tyres; we will take the next best thing". And the forecourt managers recommended the next best thing, which was whatever they had in stock. So that famous tyre-maker spent a lot of money selling other people's tyres.

Moral: Be absolutely certain, before you start to advertise, that your customers will be able to get your goods. And that you can make enough of those goods to meet the likely demand.

The pig in the poke

There was once a less than scrupulous company who had a product; they didn't make it themselves but were willing to act as selling agents. They put up the money to advertise, or maybe it was only some of the money: the proportion doesn't matter, for it was easily spent. The advertisements were full of promise, which is good, for without promise you cannot get people to buy. But the promises were *too* good and the product didn't live up to them. Having once bought the goods the customers refused to be made fools of again, and so that company not only lost all chance of repeat orders but, when they next offered a product for sale, the people said, "This company breaks its promises and we will not be deceived again".

Moral: The best way to kill a bad product is with a great advertising campaign.

Is your mousetrap better?

There are times in the best-regulated companies when a strange thing happens. A manufacturer looks at a neighbour who seems to be making a fortune, selling a good product, and thinks, "We can make that. We will sell it too and increase our own fortune". And, since there is no patent on the product, a duplicate version appears. It is copied exactly because it's exactly right, and it's priced at the same figure because that's what the market will bear. Of course the manufacturer gives it his own name and changes the colour and shape of the packet, but adds nothing else.

The manufacturer then goes to the shopkeeper and offers his wares. The shopkeeper takes a good look and thinks to himself, "But I have this product and it is selling well. I don't need a carbon copy". Except for a few shopkeepers, who like the colour of the wrapping or the fact that it comes from a company with a famous name. Those few that put the product on their shelves find customers seldom buy because they are happy with the original (which they've already used and come to trust). In the heartland of the ad-agencies, where this kind of thing happens a lot, such products are known as "me toos".

4

Moral: Don't lift a competitor's idea unless you
               can genuinely improve it. Simply cutting
               the price rarely works, because the
               competitor cuts his price too, only to put it
               up again when he's made you broke.

How to prevent an advertising disaster

It is more than likely that you are in a position where you know your
product is good, have a number of satisfied customers who come back
to you for more and all you want to do (all?) is expand your market.
In that case, most of the following won't apply to you, since you will
have asked all these questions and answered them correctly. But say
you're going into the market for the first time, with a product that is
brand new and therefore untried. How can you be sure it'll take off?
How can you be as confident about your chances of success as it's
possible to be in this uncertain world?

Be ruthlessly objective

In my experience the most common cause of failure lies in the fact
that the inventor of the product simply hasn't looked at it objectively.
It's his baby, his future glory; his judgement is temporarily blinded,
the negatives of the product are played down, the positives are built
up and before he knows where he is, he's picturing the world beating
a path to his door. What questions should the objective entrepreneur
ask? The first is, *"Will my product truly fill a need and will people
recognise that need?"*

Make genuine comparisons

Unless you're an absolute genius, someone somewhere has got a
product or service similar to yours. If you can, get one of your
competitor's products and stack it up alongside your own, with the
appropriate price tags. Then ask people whose judgement you trust
which they would buy. If they say there's nothing to choose between
them, stop. *You've got to have a benefit over an existing product to
beat it at its own game.*

Have you developed the quality far enough?

The main argument against improving the quality of what you're
selling is that it will cost you more. And so you'll have to charge more.
That's understood, but don't skimp on that additional layer of quality
which could be the difference between getting tried once and clinching

customer loyalty. Again, ask your colleagues for their views about improvements, or even go ahead slowly and test the market, being ready to make improvements as it becomes clear where they are needed. Totally new products need some advertising, based on product-benefits. You must budget for this.

Tread boldly on pricing

It's rarely a good idea to *undersell* your product. If what you're offering is both superior and distinctive (which, hopefully, it is if you've followed the rules above) surely it deserves a premium price? If you charge a penny or two more, not only will you replenish your bank balance quicker, you'll have money over for publicity. That said, if your product can't justify a higher price, and the customer can't see or experience that he's getting something better, think again. It might even be time to decide the product isn't worth backing at all, *for if you can't articulate or experience the benefits, what are you launching it for in the first place?*

What's the wrapping like?

OK, you've decided that what you offer has a plus. What about the other matters that depend on it selling: the service facilities you provide, the delivery, the maintenance, and even the colour of the pack and the kind of packaging you offer? When you create the packaging use designs and words that help to position the product in the mind of your customer. If the product is a breakthrough, can you devise breakthrough packaging for it? Often companies restrict themselves to low-cost, standard packaging and they're right to do so. But sometimes they miss a trick. Over-packaging is wrong but under-packaging is also an opportunity missed. You might actually save money on advertising *if the pack's doing the advertising for you.*

Are you offering special terms?

When you're launching a new product it can be a good idea to build into your advertising a special offer. Like a discount on orders received within 10 days. Or two for the price of one. Or buy the clock, get the battery free. Going into a new market with a product, where everyone is a non-user, *extra incentives on top of the product benefits can make your publicity work harder.*

CHAPTER ONE

Who are you talking to?

This last question is possibly the most important of all and a lot more will be said about it later. But at the start of any product launch it's very tempting to say to yourself, "I'm not a hundred per cent sure of my prime customer, so I'll get a trial where I can". This is a dangerous ploy for, as the professional marketing men will tell you, if you go for everybody you'll more often than not end up getting nobody. I'm prepared to bet that when you first started to think about making your product you had a very clear idea *who* you were making it for. But as you went along, it occurred to you that this person could also find a use for it. And so could that person. And why don't you offer it to somebody else too, just in case they want to buy. After all, you might think, you've got nothing to lose. Wrong – you've lost sight of your original market and, unless you pinpoint them directly in your advertising and publicity, you'll more than likely miss them.

Incredible though it may seem, even a product like detergent, which may at first appear to have an appeal to everyone who washes clothes, is never sold that way. One particular brand is sold only to women with front-loading washing machines, whilst another is directed to those with top-loaders. Detergent manufacturers, believe it or not, actually investigate the attitudes and lifestyles of women, find out what they wash the most frequently, how many kids they have, what their husbands do for a living, and so on. When *all* these various factors have been discovered they pinpoint the most lucrative section of that market (or the section least-well-served at that time) and create advertising that speaks *with precision and accuracy to those customers only*. I offer the information to encourage you to be absolutely clear who you're talking to.

Action checklist

You may now have the urge to advertise and can't wait to see the name of your product and company in print. You may imagine the publicity falling through the letter boxes of potential customers all round you and hope they will read your material avidly and place an order pronto. But before you set out to write your copy and visualise your pictures, ask yourself:

1. Are you offering a genuinely good product?

2. Have you some repeat sales to prove it?

3. Are you sure your customers will be able to get it?

4. Will they be able to get enough of it?

5. If it needs servicing, can you provide this?

6. Is your price right?

7. Is your packaging right?

8. Will the profit margin pay for the advertising?

9. Have you a special introductory offer to make?

10. Have you accurately defined your customer?

CHAPTER ONE

BRITAIN'S BEST-REMEMBERED ADVERTISING DISASTER

In the early 1960s Imperial Tobacco launched a cigarette named STRAND, using advertising agents S.H. Benson Ltd, who have since been absorbed into Ogilvy & Mather. "Its success," writes Mr D.H.A. Redaway (who is Imperial's Communications Manager) "was only short-lived." In fact, STRAND was a disaster. Thousands were spent on the advertising which appeared on TV, in the national newspapers and on giant billboards like the one shown here. Even today the advertising is remembered as conspicuous, intrusive and hard to get out of the mind. It did everything cigarette advertising could be asked to do, including gain trial of the cigarette, yet STRAND would not take off.

In the end the advertising was blamed, because, said the pundits, cigarette smoking was a socially acceptable habit (it was the early '60s, remember) enjoyed by gregarious people, who offered their brands freely as an aid to conversation and so on. Yet the advertising portrayed a "loner". "Quite the wrong psychology." In-depth research (I've been told) further revealed that the model in the ad was seen as homosexual. At best he portrayed solitude and rejection. The truth, however, was simpler, as the smokers who bought STRAND soon found out. It was a rotten cigarette.

C H A P T E R

WAYS TO REACH YOUR

CUSTOMERS.

A BEGINNER'S GUIDE TO

MEDIA-BUYING.

"There are nine and sixty ways of constructing tribal lays, and every single one of them is right."
Rudyard Kipling

"If you award your total advertising effort 100 points, then 60 of them must go to finding the right customer".
Michael Banks (Marketing Consultant).

CHAPTER TWO

I start by declaring a weakness: my talent lies in making advertisements, not deciding where they should appear. Media-buying is a complex and sophisticated skill and a number of excellent books have appeared on the subject, the best and most popular (I'm told) being *Spending Advertising Money* by Dr Simon Broadbent and Brian Jacobs. The work has run to many editions and has been acclaimed by one reviewer as "the best available in the English language on the vitally important task of spending £5 billion each year [in Britain]". And who am I to argue? The media scene changes all the time and I don't suppose it will be long before you're approached by the Cable TV salesman inviting you to buy time on his shows. You've probably already been approached by the rep from your local paper or radio station, or someone trying to get you to buy space in your local freesheet. All that follows here is to be treated as guidelines. Before you make your final decision you must get accurate facts and figures from the particular medium you're interested in; simply call them up and ask. That done, take soundings from your colleagues and use your own business common sense.

Local media only

In this chapter I'm not going to talk about national newspapers and giant circulation magazines; not only are such media expensive, the subject is too complex and situations change too frequently for me to say much that's helpful here. One book you will find helpful is *British Rate and Data*, which lists some 40 classifications of press media, with their names and addresses, the rates they charge for space, their audited circulations and technical specifications (in other words size of page, times when your ads must be sent in, days of publication and so on) plus telephone numbers, and in some cases a name to call for information. *Brad*, as this directory is called for short, is published monthly, and you can take out an annual subscription for £300, or buy copies singly at £115 each.* *Brad's* address is: Maclean Hunter House, Chalk Lane, Cockfosters Road, Barnet, Herts EN4 0BU, telephone 081-411 6644. If you think £115 is a bit hefty for a directory that's revised and updated every month, you should be able to find a copy in the reference section of your County Library.

* Advertised price April 1991

13

Your local radio

Independent Local Radio (to give it its proper name) began in the UK in 1973. At first it reached only 18 areas, but it has grown dramatically since then and there are now more than 79 local stations with the ability to reach between them 52% of the UK population (or 95% of the adult population). Another 30 or so commercial stations are currently being planned for each year between 1991 and 1995. Radio advertising is normally limited to a maximum of nine minutes in each hour. There is only one commercial radio station serving any one town or city, with the exception of London, which has two. Your commercial can be anything from 10 to 60 seconds long.

You're probably familiar with the broadcasts and folksy me-to-you chat peppered liberally with references to local happenings. It's used heavily by local advertisers. The main advantage is the low cost of producing commercials; it's the only medium in which you can drop a giant maraschino cherry into a lake of chocolate with a cast of thousands looking on – for the price of a commentary and a few sound effects. Also you can get on the air-waves quickly and cheaply, which is good if you have NEWS to put about. Before you use local radio, find out what audience you'll reach and what proportion that is of the local population; I can't give you figures here since they'll differ for every station. To get details on listeners and what radio time costs to buy contact the contractor who covers your area. There's just one generalisation you can make about local radio: the audience will tend to be female, younger-aged and probably down-market. But specific data, plus advertising case-histories and the cost of a package tailored to your needs, you'll get from your local station.

Your local newspaper

Advertisers spend more in the newspapers than on any other media, and the most commonly-used spaces in the broadsheet papers are 200mm across 2 columns, 250mm across four columns, 330mm across 5 columns and 380mm across six columns. Pages and half pages are also popular. You can assume 380mm across six columns is equivalent to a whole page in a tabloid; there's no space in a tabloid, however, that you can equate easily with a half-page landscape in a large-size paper.

Whether or not the local paper will work for you depends entirely on what you have to sell. *If that appeals to Joe Public,* then there's probably no more cost-effective way to reach them. But if what you have to sell is for a specialised market, say wall-plugs to builders, garden mulch to municipal and market gardeners or vending and catering equipment to offices, factories and hospitals, obviously there are more efficient and less costly ways to reach your customers.

Space-costs in local papers are based on the number of people you reach and the size of space you buy. Call the advertisement department and ask for a representative to come and talk to you. He'll explain everything: the area the paper covers, the kind of people who read it and the sizes and shapes of space you can buy. The basic unit of space is the single column centimetre and most other spaces are built up from this.

A word of warning: some newspapers can't print photographs very well, the coarseness of the newsprint causes the ink to spread and often important details can be lost. So be sure, if you supply photos to reproduce from, that they are crystal clear, the subject is simple, and (if you like) call up the rep to check that they'll come out all right.

Newspapers are especially good for announcing news, say the opening of a shop or the arrival of fresh stock, and many local retailers use them. I urge you to make the fullest use of the space representative, who although he wants you to buy space also wants to have you as an enthusiastic and satisfied customer: if your ad works it pays him, since as a local trader you'll pass the word along to your fellow businessmen.

Your local freesheet

The freesheet is the paper nobody pays for, at least readers don't pay for it, advertisers do. A freesheet runs profitably when it sells advertising and will work for you if you're selling to *Mr & Mrs Average*. Freesheets usually cost less to advertise in than ordinary papers because when people buy a paper they take the trouble to read it, but if they get it free they may toss it away unopened. What's certain is that freesheets aren't read as closely as "real" papers. Moreover, freesheets can't afford the calibre of journalist who works for a "real" paper so the quality of reporting is generally lower. "Real" papers carry more news, which makes them more interesting, which increases the readership and so the cycle goes. That said, the honest freesheet tries hard, at least to get a good "lead" story.

To advertise in a freesheet lift the 'phone and call them, they won't need a second invitation. Moreover, they will almost certainly have a service for advertisers which includes helping you write and design your advertisement and prepare the artwork. Since it's their livelihood we're talking about the service is likely to be fast and efficient, although you should check beforehand to see how much it costs. To find out how well your local freesheet works for you, try it a few times, *when you can get a good position in the paper and have a good offer to make.* One final word: *Mr & Mrs Average* put more trust in the paper they buy than the papers they get for nothing and (illogical or not) that trust rubs off on to the advertisements they see. In other words readers who believe and respect the editorial of a newspaper also tend to believe and respect the advertising the paper carries.

Your local railway station

There's a deal of variation in the size, cost and effectiveness of the sites you can buy on your local station. The posters there range from double crowns to super-sites. Many passengers wait for some time on platforms so a poster there can carry a fairly long message. Although everyone in town will use the station sometime, most of the traffic is likely to be commuters and (in coastal towns) holidaymakers. It's not common for stations to carry single advertisements for smaller companies, but I have arranged this kind of publicity, and you can either talk to the station-master, or contact the advertising department of British Rail, which is called British Transport Advertising. Other points to be made about advertising on stations are covered in the next section on poster advertising.

Local poster sites

The basic unit-size of the poster is a double crown, which measures 20 inches wide by 30 inches deep. The most widespread and popular is the 16-sheet, or if your company is in or near a new town, possibly the 4-sheet. Posters are a flexible medium in the sense that you can easily buy within your local area and not be committed nationally. However, they are inflexible in the sense that they take time to prepare and distribute to the contractors, who will paste them up and then look after them for you. Poster contractors like to have your work in their hands at least three or four weeks before it is to be shown. Normally you buy a poster for one month, but you can order it *till countermanded*, which means it will be displayed – and replaced if torn or defaced – for as long as you want it to stay up. You can, of course, change what your poster says but if you want to change it more frequently than once a month, this costs you extra.

There are around 135,000 poster sites across the country, owned by a number of different contractors, the biggest being Mills & Allen, London & Continental, Maidens and More O'Ferrall. If you see a site you especially want to use, check first to see whose name is on the hoarding, and if there isn't one, get as near as you can to the address. Then ring one of the above contractors: you'll soon find out whose site it is, how much it costs to buy for a month and when you need to have your advertising ready to despatch. At the moment there is no central poster advertising body, the British Posters consortium having been dissolved by the Monopolies Commission.

Obviously, everybody sees posters, and they let you repeat your message over and over again. The main disadvantage is that they have to communicate what you say, quickly. The poster is a medium that "he who runs may read", so clearly a long complicated message is out of the question.

Your local cinema

You can buy screen time in the cinema in four basic segments, 20, 30, 40, and 60 seconds, although other time-lengths are available if you negotiate. The advantages of the cinema are that it offers sound, colour, vision, movement and the impact of the wide screen. The disadvantage to the smaller advertiser is that unless he has available to him a "stock" film, to which he can add his own name and address at the end, production costs are very high. However, the fact that cinema ads can be bought individually, means you can create a local campaign with comparative ease, and show your commercial only in the cinemas within a fixed radius of your shop, restaurant, showroom, or whatever. You can also "time" your advertising, so if you're selling swimwear, for example, you need only appear during the late-spring, early-summer weeks.

Unfortunately it's impossible to define the audience you reach with any accuracy, since clearly it depends on the particular film showing. An audience watching a cult-art movie is likely to be quite different from one queuing for the latest John Travolta extravaganza, but as a rule of thumb you would be wise to treat the medium as principally attracting the 15–24-year-old age-group. As you will know, the normal advertising interval in the cinema consists of about ten 30-second films, many of which are "library" commercials, made for exhibition by local retailers, followed by perhaps two one-minute films created by large agencies for national advertisers. *It is a condition of contract that the films are shown with the house lights down, and the curtains opened.*

Most medium-size towns now only have one cinema although it may be divided into 3 or 4 "mini-cinemas". Cinema advertising is handled by two main contractors, Rank, for Odeon, Gaumont and Granada cinemas, and Pearl and Dean for ABC, Warner and Classic. If you want to know more, contact the manager of the local cinema and ask him to put you in touch with the advertising contractor's local sales representative. It's worth knowing that both Rank and Pearl and Dean produce "stock" films, using professional actors in appropriate settings for many types of small business. Your name and address is then added, both in sound and pictures, at the end of the film, to make it your own.

Your local buses

Probably the most widely used, and the most useful kind of bus advertising, is the side of a double decker. This takes the form of a narrow strip, some 5,300mm long by some 540mm deep, although you must not take these figures as exact since virtually every bus fleet differs. You can also use the lower panel at the back of the bus, and what are called double-fronts, one on either side of the indicator panel above the driver. Space inside is usually sold on the front bulkheads and roof panels.

The inside of a bus offers you the chance to advertise at the lowest capital cost, outside classified advertising.

Before you decide to go "on-the-buses" you must find out which garages serve which routes, and which areas the routes cover. And once your advertisement is "up", that particular bus is unlikely to change its route for some time. Good coverage depends on getting the right number of buses on the right routes. (I'm not saying a bus *can't* change routes, and even change garages – though this is unusual – I'm saying don't *expect* it to.)

What you get

The local bus fleet will give you colour, impact and good local coverage, and reaches people *as they go to the shops*. More than that, say the bus advertising salesmen, it actually *takes* them there, purses in hand. The bus companies claim they can reach 80% of all the people who live in your area in about four weeks; from then on your message continues to repeat until you decide to change it. Bus advertising is useful if you want to establish a name or slogan, and it puts you up alongside the major national advertisers, but for the local advertiser, exterior spaces are not cheap.

Most bus advertising is controlled by two companies, three if you include London Transport. The first, Primesight Ltd, claim to control most inner city buses. The second, British Transport Advertising, controls buses that run *between* the cities. For specific information talk direct to the contractors themselves. Both will design and print posters, and cards for display inside, put them up, and make sure they continue to look presentable until your advertising time runs out.

Buying colour in local press

You may be lucky and live in an area where the local newspaper has introduced the new technology, in which case colour pages will be no surprise to you. Unfortunately the great majority of local papers have not yet been able to take advantage of this new equipment, although it exists and undoubtedly makes the production of papers cheaper and quicker. Where, then, can you buy colour? The best advice I can suggest is to try and discover if you have a county magazine. If you have, it is generally printed on good art paper and can reproduce colour illustrations to a high quality. Other places to look for colour include your Chamber of Commerce Year Book, or possibly a colour magazine produced by the company that runs your freesheet paper.

Local spaces you must use

Never leave yourself out of *Yellow Pages* or *Thomson's Local Directory*. Yes, one standard entry is free in both publications, but to stand out you should buy a display or semi-display space. Don't use photographs to illustrate these spaces since they won't reproduce, but a small and simple line illustration is a good idea, and I would recommend every small business to exploit both these directories to the full.

Trade and technical magazines

Every trade, every industry, every sport, hobby, political creed, interest and profession is covered by one or more specialist magazines. The problem is there are so many that you have to be careful to pick the right ones. But the advantage to you is, if you hit the right audience, you can find your advertising is often just as interesting to them as the magazine editorial. This has led in some cases to what is known as the "controlled circulation" magazine, which isn't available on the bookstalls, but gets sent to readers through the mail. Today, some of the best trade and technical magazines are distributed in this way.

The trouble is that some trade and technical publications have not set about the task of providing the advertiser with accurate information as to who their readers are. Your answer to this is to consult the previously mentioned *British Rate and Data*, a compendium of all the newspapers and magazines available to you. Many give their audited circulation and readership figures, and thus you will know, to the nearest hundred, how many readers you get. But some do not, and you would be right in suspecting there may be good reason. There is no excuse for a magazine not to produce audited circulation figures. There will be instances where you may have a choice of as many as four or five magazines covering the same market, and this is where an insistence on hard information – from the magazine direct – is vital. Clearly, then, you use the magazines that provide you with detailed figures and not the ones that won't.

Some last thoughts on media

There are a few other places you can advertise which may not have occurred to you, but might prove beneficial. For example, if you run a sports shop, and there's a local football ground or race course, you could consider posters or a display banner for these sites. Or you may be exhibiting at some hall or conference; as well as your stand, or speakers, you might like to have your name (and stand number) big and bold on a display panel. Exhibitions are a useful way of letting customers *sample* the product, and you can also distribute inexpensive leaflets or other printed material. If you are attending an exhibition it's good advice to make your stand a worthwhile thing. This takes a lot of time and effort, but a poorly staffed stand is usually, literally, a cause of more harm than good to the exhibitor.

How much should you spend on your advertising? I'd suggest you first ask yourself what you want to do, and then find out what it'll cost you to do it, and not the other way round, which is, we have this much to spend, what can we buy with it. Somehow, if you do it that way, the tail wags the dog and you could end up spending more than you need. If you're thinking of the newspapers and local magazines, then ask yourself:

1.   Which newspapers and magazines?

2.   What size of space?

3.   How often are the advertisements to appear?

4.   On which days (months)?

5.   Featuring what products (or services)?

6.   Will you use words, pictures or both?

7.   What price are the goods and services to be advertised at?

Some examples of advertising expenditure

When I first began in the business I thought there was some foolproof scientific way to decide how much money you should spend on advertising. Recently I discovered a survey carried out in 92 consumer and industrial firms. When asked how they decided how much to spend:

*   91% used an arbitrary method of budgeting.

*   7% claimed to analyse the market situation.

*   2% used a careful method of decision making.

So you see, it's very much a hit and miss affair – what do we want to do; let's cost it out to see if we can afford it. However, to give you a guide to how firms behave in general, here's a chart which shows an average percentage of advertising expenditure against sales, for 11 different types of business, over a period of eight years.

TYPE OF BUSINESS	% OF SALES INCOME USED FOR ADVERTISING
Food	0.95%
Clothing	0.35%
Automotive	0.69%
Drink/Tobacco	1.12%
Medical/Toiletries	5.96%
Household/Leisure	1.61%
Publishing	2.05%
Tourism/Entertainment	0.75%
Retail	0.49%
Financial/Savings	0.63%
Industrial	0.47%

Source: Advertising Association.

DO YOUR OWN ADVERTISING

Advertising and promotion-
How much should you spend?

The tendency at the less sophisticated end of the market – in other words, where you are – is to spend as much (and only as much) as you can afford. Generally speaking the money you spend is directly related to the sales you make. So if you have sales of £10 million, your advertising budget could quite reasonably be £100,000; sales of £5 million could let you set aside £50,000. (You see I'm suggesting a budget of 1% of sales.) The ratio-to-sales method of deciding your budget is the tried and tested one, but if you want to get more refined, here are 10 other guidelines to consider when making recommendations.

1. The bigger the share of the market you own, the more money you spend (if you want to keep it).

2. If a lot of new products are coming into your market, you'll have to spend more to be visible.

3. If the market is growing very fast (as the computer market is today) you'll have to spend more to make an impact.

4. If your machinery (or production line) isn't working at full stretch, spend more money. If it is working at full stretch, you can (1) cut your budget, or (2) install more machines and keep spending.

5. If your product is cheap and bought frequently, the advertising budget is likely to be high, Conversely, if you make expensive "one-offs" you needn't spend much on advertising at all.

6. If a customer buys only one of your products at a time (and buys that only very rarely) you need to spend more advertising money to keep him informed (cars are a specific case in point).

7. If your product is highly priced (in other words the most expensive of its kind) you'll need to spend more to get it bought if you want a significant market share. Also, if you discount your product, or offer it with money off for a limited period, again you will have to spend disproportionately to publicise the offer.

NOTE: Cutting the price temporarily is not a way to improve sales, unless you advertise the reduction.

8. High quality products should be given big budgets. But the good thing is, superior products command a premium price, so the money to advertise them is there.

9. If you provide outstanding quality (relative to the competition) and offer it at a very good price, you don't need to do much advertising (surprise, surprise).

10. If your product is commonplace and made to pretty standard specifications, you need to spend more money to get it noticed and accepted. Conversely, custom-made products rarely need high levels of advertising.

These are the rules which many advertising agencies use when considering marketing and advertising budgets. While you shouldn't rely on *any* rules, at least these can help in making your final decision seem more scientific. Use them as a benchmark against which to evaluate your own particular position.

You can't beat the system

When the big spenders in big business choose an ad-agency, they usually make a point of visiting two or three to compare their wares. Often agencies work to a system in getting their business and describe that system to prospective customers.

At Agency No. 1 the presenter said: "Yes sir, we work to the Pyramid system." "I see", said the customer. "What's the Pyramid system?" "In our agency," came the reply, "you, the customer, come at the top of the pyramid, the service departments of the agency form the rest and, of course, we all look up to you." The customer went away to ponder.

At Agency No. 2 the presenter said: "Here, sir, we work to the Circle system." "And what's that?" "It means that you, the client, are at the centre of the circle, our workers form the ring, and we all serve you." The customer made a note and went to the third contender.

"Here", said presenter No. 3, "we work to the Mushroom system." "That one", said the customer, "is more difficult to visualise; can you tell me more?" "It's very simple really", came the reply. "Most of the time we keep our staff in the dark, but occasionally we open the door and throw manure at them."

3

TALKING TO CUSTOMERS
THROUGH THE LETTER BOX.
AND NINE WAYS TO THINK
ABOUT A MAILING-LIST.

"Of the five-or-six-hundred-odd advertisements you see every day, between seven and ten register. The rest are ignored."

Stanhope Shelton

CHAPTER THREE

It might surprise you to know that in the league table of ways to advertise, sending publicity through the mail comes third. The most money is spent on newspaper and magazine advertising, £4,806 million according to the figures when this book went to press.* Next comes TV, which gobbled up £2,286 million. Direct mail (that is, sending material through the letter box) cost advertisers £758 million. Moreover, in the last half-dozen years, the spending rate on direct mail has doubled, first because it works, and research has proved that it works, second because the cost of producing direct-mail material has increased at a far lower rate (despite the increases in postal charges) than the cost of producing advertising for any other medium.

The analogy most frequently used to describe direct mail is that whereas using other media is like taking a shotgun to your market, and peppering it with messages that might strike home or might not, direct mail is like a rifle. You can hit your target with precision and accuracy.

* Source: Advertising Association, 1989

Ways to deliver

The most obvious and widely used way to deliver letter-box material is through the mail, and the Post Office has some 250 executives dotted around their main Post Offices whose job is to help answer your questions. The man to ask for is your Postal Sales Representative, or, if there isn't one, your local Head Postmaster. He can advise you on the schemes available to make mailings simpler and cheaper, including a postage rebate if you send out more than 4,000 identical letters, a Business Reply Service, Freepost, franking machines, and even the collection of mail from you free of charge if you have a posting of 1,000 letters or more.*

Although your postman is the person most frequently used for deliveries, there are also private organisations who will undertake the job. Say you want to distribute leaflets or handbills but don't want to pay for envelopes, addressing and so on; a street-to-street contractor will help you out. Or you can put an insert in your local freesheet; that's a way to get colour into a newspaper. Or you could even trot round the newsagents in your district and come to an arrangement with them to slip your material between the pages of the morning newspapers, or regular magazines.

* Figures correct on April 1st 1991

DO YOUR OWN ADVERTISING

Spot-on timing

Talking through the letter box is a very personal way to reach your customer. Your mail-shot can be tailored exactly to your budget, and sent to people you want to do business with (unlike any other medium, where you inevitably get "wastage" readers, viewers or listeners). It's the most flexible, controllable and measurable medium available, and gives you spot-on timing. You know, for example, that everyone stocks up the drinks cabinet at Christmas. If you run a local wine store, you're going to expect good business at this time anyway, but you could put together a special Xmas deal which includes, say, a dozen reds, six whites, some port, brandy and liqueurs. If you start in good time, you can design and write your mail-piece, build your stocks up, arrange to deliver your orders, then mail (or letter-drop) a sales-piece to the well-to-do part of your district, where residents can afford to splurge a little, and have your message on the breakfast table on (say) December 1st *precisely*. Your timing, your audience, and the area in which you have to make deliveries are exactly defined.

What to send and not to send

Almost anything that's clean, legal and decent can be delivered through the letter box, I've even known of one mail-piece which included a message that appeared to be carved on a tablet of stone. (It was, in fact, a wax-based material with a marble-look.) The point to watch is cost. It isn't a good idea to send an expensive message to an audience you don't know, and which doesn't know you. If you're preparing a cheap, one-or-two-colour handbill, that's fine. Not much expense there (comparatively speaking) and no reason not to pick up orders. The time to spend big money is when you have a *definite lead*.

Expensive catalogues, samples of fabrics, and multi-page, coloured brochures are fine so long as you can be sure you've got an interested prospect. But fishing for customers is no time to be lavish. Indeed, telling the full story can actually be counter-productive in the initial stages. The first thing to do is raise the question in the customer's mind as to whether he'd like something. If he says "maybe", then mail him all the answers.

Ways to compile a mailing-list

If you decide to send sales material through the post, the hard part is putting together an address-list of the customers likely to buy. And it's harder still to be sure the list is accurate and reliable. There are

28

many ways to go about it, and a number of good books are available on the subject, not least *The Post Office Direct Mail Handbook*. The first move I would commend is to contact your local Postal Sales Representative and let him take matters from there. But what follows might be of some help in briefing you before you meet.

1. From your company files

Your company will already have one kind of mailing-list, that is your list of existing customers, with whom you do regular business and to whom you send regular invoices. Many companies today have this list on their computer; if you want to use it to send out new sales material, check it first with the help of your sales team and others who deal with customers on a day-to-day basis. Bearing in mind what your sales message is, you can then weed out people not worthwhile mailing. Some customers on your computer list may have moved, gone bust, or ceased trading for a number of reasons. Some may have bad debts, either with you or others you know about, some may have changed management teams and taken their business elsewhere, in which case decide whether it's worth trying to win them back, and if so, whether a mailing will help do that. "Clean up" the list so you're sure there's no wastage, and check you've got all the *names* right. If, say, a marketing manager has moved, make a phone call and get the name of his replacement; it's insulting to send a letter addressed to someone who left the company months ago.

2. From *Yellow Pages* and other 'phone directories

Say you want to mail all the people in your area who deal in a certain line of business. You'll find the companies listed together in the *Yellow Pages*. If you decide to go outside your local area you'll find *Yellow Pages* for the other parts of the country in a Main Post Office. Main Post Offices also hold the standard telephone directories for all parts of the UK (or should do).

3. From the Electoral Roll

Electoral Rolls can often be found in your area's main library or alternatively at the Council Offices. They give a house-by-house address list, telling you the number of people who live in each home, and their names if over eighteen years old. You'll also be able to find people living on their own (this might be useful if you're selling burglar alarms) and all the single-parent families (if you have special offers to make to them).

4. Renting a mailing-list

Many companies are happy to rent you a mailing-list, and you pick the one you go to according to the kind of list you want. The largest company of all is Dun & Bradstreet, who have lists covering 300,000 businesses, identified by their standard industrial classifications, their turnover and geographical location. Dun & Bradstreet claim their lists are updated *monthly*. You can buy from them the London Postal Districts, singly, or as many as you want at a time, and that will give you companies with turnovers of between one and five million pounds, or five and twenty millions. The cost of a thousand addresses, including the name of the managing director (and in some cases the company secretary) starts at £90.* This price is not the lowest you can find, but unlike many address-list compilers, Dun & Bradstreet are willing to sell lists as well as rent them. If you rent a list you're allowed to use it only for as many times as the renters agree – and you pay for. But if you buy a list, then you can use it for as long as you like (remembering always that it'll date if you don't continually revise it). Never cheat by renting a list, then using it for more mailings than were agreed. The lists are "seeded" to stop this and you could find yourself mailing to the secretary of the MD at Dun & Bradstreet, who'll then report back to the company that you're using their lists in an unauthorised way.

* Source: Dun & Bradstreet, April 1991

5. From professional directories

All the professions have directories which list the names, addresses and qualifications of their members. There are publishers which specialise in producing these directories, and copies of some of them are almost certain to be in your main library. So say you want to mail all architects; then you can find a complete list of them in the *Architect's Directory*. Look for the directories, too, in your Chamber of Commerce Library.

6. Contact the professional institutions

If you can't find the directory of a particular profession, get in touch with the professional institution. They will certainly have a computerised list of their members, which they may agree to sell you. They will also publish a professional news-sheet – or even a full-blown magazine – which they mail to their members. You have three options.

You can buy the address-list outright; you can buy part of the address-list, say, all the architects who live south of the Wash, or you can send the institute your sales material and ask them to "tip-it-in" to their news-sheet or magazine. A little sweet-talking with the features editor of the magazine might also earn you a mention in the editorial.

7. You can use a professional mailing house

This is where you get into the big league, for mailing houses are used to dealing with mail-outs of many thousands. Often they can do the lot for you: write, design and print your sales-message, buy envelopes, wrap any samples you might wish to send, frank the package with your own slogan or company name, and get the lot off to the Post Office. There are over 200 of these companies in the UK; some specialise in dealing with a particular section of the market – one I know is expert at reaching schools, colleges and universities – others will send to anyone, including addresses overseas. For the mailing-house best suited to your needs, take advice from the Post Office's Postal Sales Representative.

8. You can buy into a trade magazine

All the trades, indeed most businesses of any kind, have a magazine produced specially for them. You can find the address and 'phone number of the magazine you want in *Brad*. Speak to the advertising department for details about "tipping-in" publicity material. Often you can buy half the circulation if you "tip-in" whereas you have to buy it all if you use space advertising.

You can buy into someone else's list

There are two sources I have in mind. You could get in touch with one of the banks, say, Barclays, and buy space in the magazine they send out to users of Barclaycard. Or you could contact the Gas and Electricity Boards. They publish leaflets which they stuff into the bills and will probably be happy to carry your advertising in them. I don't know if the idea of being included in an unwelcome bill appeals to you, but if you're lending money, there could be worse places to advertise.

To summarise

This is *not* a comprehensive chapter of ways to compile a mailing-list; the subject is complex, and this book is about helping you produce advertising *material*. But it should give some preliminary suggestions so that when you get down to discussing specifics you have at least a rough outline of the alternatives. I would like to stress that your mailing-list is a key component in any campaign talking to customers through the letter box. To quote Geoff Longbottom, a highly respected Direct Marketing consultant: "Even a badly produced mail-shot sent to the right list can produce good business, but the best-designed and produced mail-shot sent to the wrong list will be a disaster".

C H A P T E R

4

EVERYTHING YOU NEED
TO KNOW BEFORE YOU CAN
DO GOOD ADVERTISING

"There are three ways to produce great advertising,
1. Work 2. Work 3. Work."
                    Bill Thompson, Agency Creative Director

"Nothing is more humiliating than to see idiots succeed
in enterprises we have failed in".
                                        Flaubert

CHAPTER FOUR

Previously we have considered the questions: Are you ready to advertise? Which media will you find most useful? How can you reach customers without wastage? I hope you don't expect, in this chapter, to be able to roll up your sleeves and get down to creating advertisements. There's some way to go before we start to discuss actual advertising techniques. Bill Thompson (above) says you need to do three things; they are:

1. Get to know *all* about your product or service.

2. Get to know *all* about your competition.

3. Get to know *all* about your customers.

The best way to end up in despair, wondering how anyone ever managed to produce effective selling in print, is to attempt the task before you've prepared yourself. The way I like to put it when I lecture newcomers in the copywriting business is: do your homework first. What do I mean by that; what are the moves to make before you start to write and draw? I intend it as no slight when I ask:

Do you really know everything about your product or service?

I think it would help you if I described how *I* set about preparing to write an advertising campaign. Firstly I make it my job to get to know the company, and that would most certainly include visiting the factory or workshops. I go onto the factory floor and watch the product *being made*. I start at the beginning of the production line, finding out what materials are used, and what their technical names are. I follow the product through every stage, and note the number of stages there are. I speak to the people working at every stage, find out what they do and why such-and-such a screw, clip, cotter pin or bolt is better than another kind. I ask about the strength and durability of the materials, and try to discover what this company does that's different from the way their rivals work. Do they have as many work-stages, as many people making the product, as carefully, conscientiously, and efficiently? I ask how much experience the workforce have, how long they've been doing the job, what qualifications are necessary, how they learned their skills. At the end of my visit I have a list of all the facts, figures and data that have been mentioned throughout the journey. Much of it might seem irrelevant initially, some of it will inevitably end up omitted from the finished work, but during the

35

preparatory stage everything, down to the last detail, I treat as important.

Talking to the man in charge

When I've gleaned as much information as possible from the work-force, and am completely *au fait* with the stages of production, I speak to the factory manager. The questions I like to ask him are about the philosophy behind the way he runs the place. What are his priorities, what emphasis does he put on speed of production, efficiency and cost-cutting and how does he solve contradictions that may arise between making the product fast and ensuring quality is maintained? Clearly he has to reconcile his duties as a production expert responsible to the company with his duty to turn out the best possible goods for the customer. Most important for me is to gauge his *attitude*, which, if it's the right one, could give me an angle to write about when it comes to discussing quality control, inspections, number of items rejected per production-batch and so on, all of which information is useful when reassuring customers they are buying the best. Once again, the keynote of any discussion is the facts, how many inspectors there are, how many inspection procedures, the number and kinds of quality checks, who makes the final decision that the product shall be released, what criteria have to apply before a particular item is rejected, who has the final say.

To give you an idea of the depth I like to go into, let me tell you about a visit to a well-known shoe company. Armed with my notebook, I watched a pair of shoes being made, from the time the sole was stamped out of two-inch-thick cow hide by a 20 ton press, until the final stage where the company insignia was laid on the inner-sole in 22 carat gold leaf. Altogether there were some 200 operations, many carried out by hand, and the men making the shoes were – for the most part – elderly skilled craftsmen. The plain result was that the shoes were very expensive, and part of my task was to convince potential customers that they were worth the price. I wrote an advertisement, of some 400 words, in a style that made it seem to be written by the company chairman, who was no mere figure-head but worked hard at his desk. After he approved the final artwork, he took me aside, and admitted with a grin that the advertisement had told him things about the way his shoes were made which he either *didn't know or had forgotten*. The campaign ran, and proved successful, but it would have been impossible to write without this vital information.

After the workforce, the sales force

My next task is to speak to the men and women who go out and sell your goods. That is your representatives, demonstrators, engineers, or whoever. What I want them to tell me is *how they do it*. Who better than your sales force know the promises that pull most weight, the facts and figures that most impress buyers, the strengths your product has over rivals, the weaknesses it has, what buyers like best about it and why, what models sell best and why? I also ask about pricing policy. How do your prices compare with your competitor's? Do rivals ask for more, and if so why? Or less, and if so why? And when a sales team is confronted with criticisms of the product how do they answer those criticisms? What reasons are most effective in persuading customers that a high price is worth paying? Or if the price is low, how do they reassure buyers the quality isn't? I consider I've prepared myself adequately to present the case in advertising only when I've asked every question and answered every doubt about what is being made, the way it's made and why it's made and priced like it is. What I'm describing here is not an exceptional discipline, carried out on rare occasions, it is standard practice in good advertising agencies. I would be very dubious about setting to write advertisements, until fully armed with the above information. Nor do I think this is the end of the enquiry. The next thing to ask is:

Do you really know enough about the competition?

To set about this task, I first visit the shops where the product is sold. Here I physically compare it with everything produced by rivals, and make what I like to call the 'side-by-side' test. I stack up the benefits the goods offer against those provided by rival goods displayed. I talk to assistants and ask them to tell me about their stock. Which models offer which features? Why are some better than others, what especially appeals to them about goods I have to advertise and what doesn't appeal? Then I ask one of the salespeople to actually *sell* me the product. And I have a notebook handy, to record everything said. If the shop people are professionals they know all the facts and figures, what has sold the product to previous customers, what the complaints ratio is, what the delivery record is like, how the after-sales service stacks up. And finally, I ask about reputation.

I don't feel happy leaving the retailer until I have in my mind's eye the position the goods hold in the market, in relation to other goods available. I seek out strengths, probe suspected weaknesses, and press for attitudes on value-for-money, reliability of performance, expected life-cycle, and quality of after-sales service.

Now for your rival's sales literature

Since the eventual outcome of all this searching is to prepare sales literature, I want to see all the sales material produced by other companies in the same field. I set about this in several ways.

1. Respond to their advertising by completing coupons which offer to send brochures.

2. Telephone for sales literature from companies not currently advertising.

3. Collect as much rivals' literature as I can from retail outlets.

4. Read the trade press to see how rivals advertise to buyers in the trade.

Allowing for a reasonable time to elapse for all this material to arrive, I then set about a study of it. The initial impressions are the first things I note. Is the material of good quality, did it arrive in good time, did it impress me, did I *want* to read it? Next, the actual reading-process. Is the material well written and easy to assimilate? Do I enjoy reading it, and if so, why? Do I believe what it tells me? At what level of intelligence is it aimed?

Most intelligent people ignore advertising because most advertising ignores intelligent people

At the end of this period I not only know where "my brand" stands in the market compared to others, but also how the others react to an enquiry about their products. Do they respond quickly, and seem keen to make a sale? What additional follow-up is there after sending their material? Do they tell me *what to do* at the end of reading about their product? Finally I make a list of all the claims rivals make, and what points they consider most important in convincing me that theirs is the best model to buy. That way I hope to know which rival companies are most likely to make a sale after receiving a direct enquiry. The last question I address myself to is:

Do you really know everything about your customers?

This area, I regret to say, is where the smaller business is at a disadvantage compared to the giant company who can call on the services of an advertising agency. Because an ad-agency can afford to carry out market-research into who buys the products their clients offer for sale. Nonetheless, there are obvious areas you can look at:

1. What sex are your customers?

2. What age?

3. Where do they live?

4. What do they earn?

5. How large are their families?

6. How frequently do they buy what you offer?

In the end I expect to be able to picture a single man (or woman) *who epitomises your typical customer.* I know his age, salary, and attitude to life, what he most wants from a product like yours, and the amount he is prepared to pay to get what he wants. I expect to be able to stand in front of him, and sell him the product man to man. I hope to be able to anticipate the questions and objections he'll raise, and have my answers ready for him. I know the way to talk to him, the tone of voice to use, the level of technicality or sophistication to speak at. And when I finally settle down to write, I write to an individual, one man, and I write *directly* to him. Because I believe if you know your customer, have a clear picture of him, understand his nature and his needs, and what makes him laugh, wince, agree and disagree, you're in a stronger position to persuade than you ever are if you simply write to some vague category of being who may or may not be out there, and who may or may not want to know.

When the homework is done

I do not in any way underestimate the time and trouble it will take you to do all I have described in this chapter. I also appreciate that the effort is generally outside your existing duties and you may find it difficult to put the discipline into practice. Obviously you will delegate; for example the search for rival sales literature can be given to a reliable junior or even your secretary. You could simply make a list of all the companies you need to know about and ask to have their advertising material on your desk by a certain date. But what I would ask you *not* to do is leave yourself short of ammunition in what is going to be nothing more or less than a sales-battle. You are going to sell in print, against people who have no compunction in taking business from you. You are going, in the end, to have to commit yourself to certain costs. To skimp on the preparatory work is cheating no one but yourself. The more effort you apply at this stage, the less you need apply in the next. And even now, I do not want you to settle down to write.

First I recommend a cooling-off period, during which you allow all the information you've gathered to settle in your mind. Perhaps you could forget about the whole matter of making advertising for a couple of weeks, while the details are re-forming themselves silently in your subconscious. You can pull the picture up occasionally to review it, think about certain aspects, establish priorities, discard details you feel don't matter. But give yourself a period in which to *think*, maybe even talking things over with colleagues, commenting on your advantages and how to convey them most vividly, and your disadvantages and how you can answer them when they raise themselves in customers' minds. In a sentence, forget advertising for a while, and turn your attention to something else.

DOING YOUR HOMEWORK

A CHECKLIST

About your product or service.

1 Go onto the factory floor.
2 See the product being made.
3 Talk to the workforce.
4 Talk to the Production Director.
5 Talk to the sales force.
6 Find what they think are the main sales points.
7 And the main negatives.
8 And how they answer the negatives.

About the competition.

1 Go to the shops.
2 Talk to the sales staff.
3 Compare everything on display.
4 Get the salesperson to sell you your product.
5 See what they like about it.

6 And what they dislike.
7 Collect all your rivals' sales literature.
8 See how it's followed up.
9 Pinpoint your most dangerous rival.

About your customers.
1 What sex are they?
2 What age are they?
3 Where do they live?
4 What do they earn?
5 What are their principal needs?
6 And their principal worries?
7 How frequently do they buy?
8 Would they buy your product again?
9 How much would they pay?
10 Are they satisfied with your back-up services?
11 Can you visualise *one* customer and write to him or her specifically?

C H A P T E R

5

TOUCHSTONES TO HELP YOU
WRITE GREAT HEADLINES.

*"The visual person is always at the mercy of the writer.
You see a picture of a little old man in National Health
glasses entitled 'This man carved Pinocchio', and you
think 'What a sweet old man'. But put 'This is a German
War Criminal' and immediately it becomes something
else".*

David Bailey

CHAPTER FIVE

Your period of preparation is over. The time has come to get down to *writing*. And make no mistake, the writing comes before the pictures. If you're wise, you'll start with the very basics. Pick a day when you've got plenty of time and are unlikely to be disturbed. Pick a place where you'll get peace and quiet and ask your secretary to keep interruptions to a minimum. Bring in a couple of artist's A3 layout pads (honestly, it somehow feels different to have large virgin sheets ready for your immortal prose). Have some easy-rolling pens to write with. Put the product you're selling on your desk. Or, if that is impractical, get some photographs of it to put on your desk. Have handy the file of all your competitor's literature which you've spent the last week or so putting together. Make sure you're in a writing mood, not looking on the job as a chore, but rather as an interesting challenge you're going to enjoy. Your enthusiasm is high and your brain isn't suffering from a "Monday" feeling, or a hangover from the night before. Good, now, what are you looking for?

You're looking for a promise

Not what your product *is*, but what it *does* for the buyer. Not how it came to be, but what it provides in terms of benefits. A great headline is all *promise*. It's the heart of your reason for being in business. Look, you're going to say, I offer you something you really shouldn't be without. It's a terrific product at an excellent price. It'll improve your life so you'll never want to part with it. And you shouldn't buy it from anyone else but me.

How to find the promise: A system

It's unlikely that there is only one reason to buy your product or service; there may be half a dozen. What you have to do is pick the best, the most persuasive. Here's how. You know those contests that appear in magazines (or on the back of cereal packets) where you're given a list of good things about, say, a holiday in the Bahamas and you have to put them in the order of most importance? And if you hit on exactly the right order, you win the holiday? That's the thing you should do next. Take all the things your product or service will do for people, and make a list. Include everything you can think of. Start with the most obvious, but go right on down to the details. Include your after-sales service if that is applicable. If you can offer a money-back guarantee, add that to your column. When you've racked your own brains on all the benefits, check through your competitors' literature. Is there anything there you can steal? Don't be afraid to steal. I don't mean write out the promises in the exact words your rivals use. But, at the same time, don't let them out-sell you with enticements and advantages which you can fairly offer. Below I've made up a list from an imaginary company, THE LOCAL STEEL COMPANY. The list is in no particular order, it's just a summation of everything they can do to please their prospective customers. Use my list as an aid when compiling your own. Remember, you're looking for *benefits*.

THE LOCAL STEEL COMPANY LTD

LIST OF BENEFITS
You hold types of steel nobody else does.
You can deliver it anywhere, in days.
You can shape and finish it any way the customer wants.
It comes in many different grades.
You've got many different saws to cut it.
You can saw it into squares, discs and blanks.
You have some imported special steels.
You have engineers as salesmen.
You do carbon-free welding.
You've got 24 inspectors to see the work is right.
You've got government contracts.
You've a fleet of your own trucks.
Your prices are fair, for the service you give.
You work at top speed; no waits, no disappointments.
Your customers are willing to speak for you (ask them to, then quote them).
You produce free literature.
You offer an advisory service, on site.
You reach customers within a 100-mile radius of your factory before anyone else in the trade.
You will guarantee everything; materials, workmanship and delivery.
The MD will personally investigate complaints.
You've got 10 new items this month.
Now add your complete address.
Your full telephone number(s).
Your fax number.
The name of at least one person to contact.

Finally, write down what you want the customer to do.

When your list is complete

You're happy you've got down every reason why your customers should buy? You're sure you've got a complete list? Fine, now I want you to re-arrange that list so you've got your benefits *in order of importance*. What should you consider important? Only you know that for sure, but here are some pointers.

* Do you have any benefit that is exclusive to you?

* Is the product or service new?

* Is it a step forward in its field?

* Do you do anything quicker, cheaper, safer, or more effectively than your competitors can?

* Are you offering anything (such as a catalogue) free?

If you've ever been a salesman, you'll have a gut-feeling about the main advantages of your product over the competition. You can't have got this far in business without having a sixth sense about the real appeal of your goods. Bring that sense into play now. Don't imagine you are writing an advertisement, imagine you are talking to the prospect face to face; often this can take the terror out of advertising copy. After all, a headline is only selling *in print*, the principles don't change. You don't write something on paper that you wouldn't happily say to your prospect in person. You're not trying to be a literary giant, you're trying to persuade. You have to be an advocate. Remember, what you want now is *the most important benefit you can offer your customer*. It need not be just one benefit, it can be a combination of reasons. But you need to be able to express them in a pithy, and preferably not-too-long headline. Set to work on picking from that list you've made of all the benefits the ones most advantageous to your customer. Once you're absolutely sure about this, then you have the substance of the main headline for your advertising.

Now think about who you're talking to

Up till now you've been thinking about your product or service, and all the things you can say about it. From that number of reasons-to-buy, you have selected the main reason-to-buy. Your common sense, your knowledge of the market, and your study of your competitors' products and literature have convinced you it's the right thing to major on in your publicity. Now stop thinking of *what you're writing about*, and start thinking about *who you're writing to*. Again, let's go back to the absolute basics.

* Is your customer a man or woman?

* How old is he/she?

* How rich/poor is he/she?

* Can you see your customer in your mind's eye?

* Can you imagine speaking to him/her personally?

* What are his/her hopes, needs, likes, dislikes?

There can be a tendency, when you are writing advertisements, to forget basics like this, and be carried off into a dreamworld, remembering the ditties from TV commercials, or the headlines from witty posters you've seen around town with their clever plays on words. And when this happens, the writer is tempted to come up with puns, jokes, or twisting well-known phrases and sayings to apply to the product for sale. Please don't do this. It takes you away from the reality of selling into indulging your own skill with words. The idea is not to make the customer smile, the idea is to sell like blazes. And to do that you have to appeal to a basic need. Never forget, while you're in your office away from distractions, you're still a salesman. And you're talking to someone who knows you're going to ask them to part with money. They're serious, so should you be.

What if you're selling a service?

Previously, when I asked you to make a list of everything you had to offer, I used as an example a specific range of products. It could be, however, that you don't have any product to sell, instead you're providing a service. You might clean windows, clothes or carpets. You might cook food for special occasions. You might be a solicitor, an accountant or shopkeeper. More and more companies are setting up these days with nothing to offer but their own skills, talents and energies. Your approach to writing your advertising should be no different from companies that have products. Take my own business, for example, the advertising industry; all advertising agents sell a service. They have no product to speak of, the only things they actually *produce* are bits of paper and reels of film with words and pictures on them. Moreover, there are over 600 agencies up and down the country offering to produce bits of paper and reels of film. They have to devise ways of making themselves different and offering their customers something special.

If you want to keep it simple, and keep your thinking straight, stick to the system. Draw up a list of benefits. Put down the advantages you can offer your customers, not forgetting to check rival literature to make sure you've got them all. Then work out the order of importance, remembering that a service that operates with a unique promise, but in the north of Scotland, say, could well provide you with an opportunity to offer the same promise in the south of England. And never be afraid to *think*. Nothing can be a substitute for real thinking about your company, and while you're doing it you might come up with an aspect you've never considered before. If you do, terrific, maybe you can include it in your company's plans. There's nothing wrong with improving your service before you spend money on advertising. Here's the list of advantages offered by my imaginary agency, SELLEM QUICK ADVERTISING.

SELLEM QUICK ADVERTISING

LIST OF BENEFITS

You already have 50 blue-chip customers.

Your staff are the best in their field.

You have a lot of case-histories that can prove your service is terrific.

You have many years of experience.

You will call on your clients and give them a detailed explanation of what you do.

You have a fresh attitude: most people zig when they do a job; you zag. (In other words, you produce the unexpected.)

You're very successful.

You offer a wide range of services.

You can make your customer's money go further.

You can show examples of the work you've done for others.

Prospective clients are welcome to call and look you over.

If you haven't got something your clients want you'll get it in days.

If something needs expert care and treatment you have (or can find) exactly the expert needed.

You're very handy to reach.

You're utterly reliable.

And everyone in your business is cheerful and nice to know.

Now add your complete address.

And your telephone numbers.

And your fax number.

And your branch offices.

The name of at least one person to contact.

Finally write down what you want the customer to do.

Writing the crucial headline

Even after all my time in the business, I still sweat over headlines. I spend more time working on them than on any other part of the advertisement, because I know I've got just moments to capture the attention of my reader. If my headline gets him, then I should have the skill to keep him with me. But if I miss him, I know I'll never get another chance.

A long time ago, someone told me I had about 1½ seconds to say to my prospect, "I've got something for you". After that, he'd either throw my leaflet away, or (if I was writing an advertisement) turn the page. That may be a slight exaggeration. You may well have two seconds. But not much longer, so you've got to get it right. I've been hammering home, for the last few pages, the importance of making a promise. What other guidelines can I give you? (And please remember, they are guidelines: the golden rule is, there are no golden rules in advertising.)

1. Make your headline clear. I mean crystal clear. Your prospect must understand at once what your offer is. So be simple, specific and direct. Don't be coy or beat about the bush. Lay the promise firmly on the line.

2. Don't be clever. When the ad-agency for Heineken first wrote the line: "Heineken refreshes the parts other beers cannot reach", there was hardly a soul in the building who understood it. Yes, they went on to put millions of pounds behind it, and today it's a catch-phrase. Remember, you haven't got millions of pounds.

3. Avoid long words. Stick to simple Anglo-Saxon, rather than words derived from Latin or Greek. There's a short word in English for virtually every long one, and if you think hard enough, you'll find it.

4. No high-technology please. Even if what you're selling is complex or scientific, don't try to explain how a thing works in a headline. Instead, explain what it does for the reader.

5. Length doesn't matter. Or rather, it doesn't matter very much. Some people think that short pithy headlines work better than wordy ones. That's a reasonable thought. No headline should be over-wordy. But *what you say* is what matters.

6. Use real facts and figures. Truth sells; puffs and exaggerations don't. A promise made up out of your own head *cannot* be as effective as the truth about the product.

7. Be wary of adjectives. Exciting, amazing, incredible and other superlatives rarely manage to impress. If you really are offering a breakthrough product, it's enough to explain the breakthrough. The news will work for you. Adjectives, more often than not, slow communication rather than speed it.

8. Be colloquial. This helps because it makes you sound human and relaxed. It means you are talking to your customer rather than shouting at him. Most customers are perfectly sane and intelligent. If what you say is sane and intelligent, you'll be heard.

9. Don't exaggerate. It stops you being believable. And credibility is important. If you think the phrase would raise a smile of disbelief if you said it to someone, it'll get a mental guffaw if you write it.

10. Check it out. When you think you've finally got the immortal line, don't just lie back and relax. Ask someone about it. Say: "Do you think you'd be interested in a product that does this? Would you consider buying it?" And accept their answer.

What if the headline won't come?

Let's say you've observed all the rules, and you've been penning for some time to no avail; what then? Well, here is a trick I sometimes try. Forget the headline altogether. Go on and write some of the text of the advertisement – what is known as the "body copy". This should be easy because of the time you've spent preparing yourself, and getting the benefits into the right order of importance. Let your pen flow freely. Keep the sentences short, and make each one contain some new point or other. Don't repeat yourself, but keep up a reasoned argument for the product.

If your experience is anything like mine, this is quite an enjoyable exercise, and since your mind becomes more relaxed, your writing will become relaxed. When you've got down the case for the defence, so to speak, read it over to yourself. You could easily find that somewhere in the body copy you've got a sentence, or perhaps even a phrase, which gives you the ideal headline. Because you weren't trying so hard, the words *arrived*.

Another trick to try

Delve back into the files where your competitors' literature is kept. Read through some of their headlines. And their body copy. Perhaps down in the small print, where many people fail to go, there's a little nugget which you can polish up and turn into salesman's gold. If you're experienced in selling, you must know the lines *you* use that really hit home. The words that make the prospect stop and think. The one or two "clinchers" which, when you come out with them, you can tell instinctively have made an impression. Is there a headline in any of those?

A ditty that may help

When I first began in the business I went through agonies trying to compose headlines my boss would accept. I often used to wonder whether some of the things I had to sell contained any benefit to the customer at all. He soon scotched that one. "Look son, take it from me, there's a promise in every product. *Every* product. If you want to write advertising that sells, find it". And then he'd say:

> *"Tell me this, and tell me true,*
> *Or else my lad, to hell with you,*
> *Less how the product came to be*
> *And more of what it does for me!"*

With that ditty ringing in my ears I slipped out of his presence to continue the search for gold. This is the point at which you must avoid despair; once you've cracked this bit, the rest comes easy. The strict discipline of searching for a promise convinced me of one thing, which has been proved by the sales results, over and over again.

You won't find an effective headline until you find something effective to say

I'm talking about the meaning of words. The content. Not the *way* you say it, which may or may not sound clever, but the actual substance. You must have a good promise to make, or you'd be out of business by now. Remember, you're inviting someone to trade, offering something they'll enjoy owning and using. You're looking to answer a specific need which you know they have. All you need do in a headline is tell the customer how he stands to gain. Dear Mr or Mrs Customer, here's what's in it for you.

Some useful words to use

Everybody in advertising knows there are certain words called "buzz" words. They help to move people into action. There aren't many of them, and they're used over and over again, but don't let that worry you. We use them so often because we know they work. A cliché becomes a cliché because it's a very good way of saying something. Here are some of them:

Introducing	Money off
Announcing	Unrepeatable offer
New	For a limited time only
Just released	Offer closes on (date)
Exclusive	Save pounds
Special Offer	Secret
Free	Challenge
Unique	Breakthrough
For the first time in Britain	Guarantee
Never before	Direct from the makers
Bargain	A major step forward in (what-
Economy	ever)

Two final points to check

Let us assume that with much sweat and blood you've at last got that form of words which expresses your promise as clearly and interestingly as it can be said. Congratulations. If it took you a long time, that's nothing to worry about, it takes every good copywriter a long time, no matter how experienced he is or how often he's been faced with a similar job. Believe me, your effort will be repaid in sales so never regret the work you put in on headlines.

One of my old bosses told me he believed anyone with the nous to string two words together should be able to write body copy (not entirely true) but it took a craftsman to come up with an effective headline. Now there are just two other checks you can make.

1. Have you written it in the present tense?

You probably have, because it's the most natural way to write anyway, but just check. "Was" becomes "is". "Look how it will bring up paintwork" becomes "Look how it brings up paintwork". And so on.

2. Have you crossed out the present participle?

"Watch your sales going through the roof" becomes "Watch your sales go through the roof". "The greatest way of saving yet" becomes "The greatest way to save yet".

These two principles, writing in the present tense and avoiding the "ing" whenever possible are good rules of thumb whenever you write advertising or publicity. There may be the odd time when an "ing" cannot be avoided but generally it's just a matter of hard thought and continued application. Look all the time for clarity and simplicity, for the colloquial form and friendly tone of voice. You want sweet reason and calmness rather than the hectic, frenetic, tub-thumping style. The customer is a reasonable soul, he'll give you his attention and respect. Use facts and figures. Tell the truth. Remember, finally, that when all the fancy pencil-work is done, a great headline doesn't depend on the *way* you make your promise. It depends on the promise you make.

CHAPTER FIVE

Finding the right words

A Checklist

1. Have you done your homework?
It's no good sitting down to write until you have
all the facts at your command.

2. Have you bought your materials?
To see things afresh, get some A3 layout pads
and free-flowing pens. It makes you *feel* right.

3. Have you allowed yourself the time?
You're not going to be able to concentrate
unless you're free of appointments,
interruptions and have got the "space" to work.

4. Are you following the system?
A disciplined way of working produces the right
results. Haphazard effort means you forget
things, and end up not seeing the wood for the
trees.

5. Are you writing the way you speak?
No great literature or funny puns. No clever
aping of what you imagine advertising to be.
Be simple, direct, colloquial.

6. Can you "see" your customer?
Think of who you're talking to. Write what
they want to hear. Say what's in it for them.

7. Have you found the promise?
Single out the main benefit for your customer.
Then make the offer the most attractive way
possible, using only the facts.

8. Have you checked out your solution?
Don't be satisfied you understand what you're
saying. Make sure everyone else understands
too.

FIFTY ADVERTISING HEADLINES
THAT FORCED ME TO READ ON

When I sit down to write a headline, I find it helps to get into the mood if, before I start, I read through a few. Below I've collected fifty of them, examples of ads I've seen which forced me to move on, into the story. The secret of a good headline is that it contains an intelligent thought. Then, all that happens is that you use the fewest words to convey the greatest meaning. Remember, the power of a headline rests partly in the way the words have been phrased, but depends mostly on how interesting it makes your message sound.

1. How to get your money back when completely satisfied
(This is a version of 50p off. But you get the 50p when you mail back the wrapper, after you've bought and eaten the product.)

2. If your butcher's meat costs less than this, it's probably worth it.

3. To people who think all the great little country inns are in other parts of the country.
(An ad in a local paper, suggested how easy it was to ignore the good places on your own doorstep.)

4. Last Summer, the leading sun lotions were sent to Harvard University Medical School. What were the lessons?
(The story explained how Piz Buin Sun Lotion came out best in all the medical tests.)

5. The finest designers from the four corners of the world, can be found on our corner.
(Ad for new, high-fashion shop on corner of the High Street.)

6. Wines you can sink your teeth into.

7. If you live in a house that's five years or older, you're probably living with a thief.
(Ad explained the importance of insulation, and that only the very latest homes have it.)

8. What some of my competitors call fresh, isn't fresh to me.
(Ad for a greengrocer careful to bring from the market only the best.)

56

9. Nature says the first day of Spring is on March 21st. The Dutch say it's a cold grey day in Winter.
(Ad sold indoor bulbs that would bloom in December.)

10. On a motorbike you can only make one mistake. We promise you won't make it here.
(Ad for a motorbike accessory and repair shop, which promised they never fit the wrong product, nor fit it badly.)

11. What it means in thrills, trophies and deep contentment to come fishing in Canada.

12. How to read a banana.
(Ad for a greengrocer's shop, about how to tell whether a banana is fresh and ripe by "reading" marks on its skin.)

13. The 18-week Charles Atlas course as paid for by H.M. Government.
(Ad explained how joining the army makes you fit.)

14. Can you see why one watch costs £140 more? The country's leading watch experts can't.
(Ad compared two 18ct gold dress wrist-watches.)

15. Come where oysters grow on trees and ships founder on mountains.
(Ad explained some of the strange sights to see in Jamaica.)

16. The best parts of our bikes are held on with string.
(Ad for Halford's cycle shops, where each bike had a low price-tag on.)

17. There's so much pork in this Sainsbury's sausage, maybe you should try it with apple sauce.

18. Wouldn't you like more than just money for a week's work?
(Ad for The Army, emphasising esprit-de-corps.)

19. You may have the strength to arrest criminals. But have you the personality to arrest crime?
(Ad to recruit police cadets, asking for intelligence and good character.)

20. Where would the British Farmer be without the Land Rover? £1,000 better off!
(Ad sold a farm truck with all the Land Rover features, at £1,000 less.)

21. Even if you're over 30, your skin is only 3 weeks old.
(Ad for face cream, explained how skin constantly renews itself.)

22. How to turn the room in your head into a room in your home.
(Ad explained how a wallpaper and paint shop can make your ideas come true.)

23. If you're quite sure you can do this job, please don't apply.
(Ad recruiting people to care for the mentally handicapped.)

24. This fully fitted kitchen, direct from the makers, only £2,000. A comparable kitchen from elsewhere costs at least £900 more.
(Cost comparison ad for fitted furniture. This kind of direct comparison is now illegal, unless you name the brand compared.)

25. What do they say about you behind your back?
(Ad explained how patients said terrific things about nurses, when talking from bed to bed.)

26. Your antifreeze will freeze before our oil will.
(Ad explained a new grade of oil, and emphasised its advanced development. It's hard to sell motor oil.)

27. Don't buy two turkeys for Christmas.
(Ad explained how to choose good wine and not end up with a dud bottle – i.e. a "turkey".)

28. The most unforgettable meal I ever made.
(Ad for chilli showed picture of diner with flames shooting from mouth.)

29. The Yoghurt with too much fruit.
(Testimonial from aesthetic who didn't believe yoghurt should contain fruit.)

30. There has never been a better reason to watch television
(Ad showed letter from patient cured of breast cancer, after being examined by a new method featured in the television programme.)

31. If your child brings home bad school reports, he could be another Einstein.
(Einstein was nicknamed Mr Dullard as a child, due to a learning disability.)

32. Mandatory retirement isn't mandatory for everyone.
(Ad featured 37 US presidents who held office after they were over 65.)

33. A machine that screams for help when your child can't.
(Ad featured electronic-eye alarm which rang if a child fell into the swimming pool.)

34. Why should companies stop making disappointing cars? You're still buying them.
(Ad featured survey of buyers disappointed with their cars.)

35. There's never been a shortage of the energy that powers our cars.
(Ad for toy cars pictured energetic children.)

36. And you thought Wales was the pits.
(Ad explained only 6% of Welsh workforce mine coal.)

37. Who says the good die young?
(Ad featured piano, still excellent after many years.)

38. See how they don't run.
(Ad featured non-drip paint.)

39. They're so tender you can eat them with your lips.
(Ad for corn-fed chicken.)

40. After playing for 200 hours non stop, a vital part of this Hi Fi failed.
(Vital part was person controlling hi fi who stayed awake for 200 hours for Guinness Book of Records.)

41. A testimonial for this washing machine from four people who've never used it in their lives.
(They were an electrician, an enameller, an insulation expert and a steel technician.)

42. Like this coat? The last owner was shot in it.
(Ad showed a real leopard-skin coat.)

43. What if they only gave blood to people who were donors?
(Ad to people who've not yet given blood.)

44. If you have the talent, we have the theatre.
(Ad for nurses, showing operating theatre.)

45. Where else can three minutes' work last a lifetime?
(Another ad for nurse-recruitment, showing patient whose heart had stopped.)

46. Could you use a small percentage of £16,000,000,000?
(Ad offered commission to agents who could persuade people to open savings accounts. Annual amount saved by small savers is around £16 bn.)

47. On April 24th, Argentina attacked Great Britain with one of the world's most sophisticated weapons.
(Ad which ran during the Falklands crisis, showed rolled-up newspaper being brandished like a weapon.)

48. Which twin is 5 years younger?
(Ad explained how non-smoker, non-drinker is allowed 5 years on life assurance premiums.)

49. Goodbye Yves St Laurent, Pierre Cardin, Nino Cerruti. Hello Oscar de la Renta.
(Ad introduced new fashion designer on a par with greats but currently unknown.)

50. How to get your children stuck into a book instead of glued to the television.
(Ad for children's book club.).

One last thing I'd like to point out about headlines, now you've read 50 good ones. Did you notice there were very few *short* headlines, and no puns? Although there were juxtapositions between words and pictures (as in "one of the world's most sophisticated weapons", where the illustration was a rolled-up newspaper). Research has shown longer headlines actually gain more readership than short ones, provided they're *saying* something. I hope this list puts you in the mood to produce something equally pithy for your business.

Tale of a shirt

One day, a shirt-maker called on an advertising agency to show them a new shirt. This shirt, said the maker, is good cotton, washes nicely, irons well, feels good on the skin, has single cuffs, mother-of-pearl buttons, the tail is long enough to stay tucked in the trousers, and I can make it at a great price. Will you advertise it for me, please?

The agency looked at the shirt and saw that it was good. But they also saw it was virtually identical with twenty other shirts already on the market. Leave it with us for a month, they replied, and we'll see what we can do.

Enter the shirt-maker four weeks later, hoping to see a great advertising campaign. Instead he saw a new shirt. This one was made of *pure silk*. The collar was rounded. The cuffs were doubled and rounded. It had a fly front, hiding the row of buttons, and making it perfect to wear with a bow tie. It was packed in a black box, in black tissue paper (this made the off-white silk look pure white). And all the pins and pieces of paper and plastic that normally make a new shirt the very devil to unpack had disappeared.

This isn't my shirt, said the shirt-maker. No, said the agency, but can you make one like it? Because this shirt is unlike any other shirt in the country – the Rolls Royce of shirts. It's singular, and it makes you singular. More important – *it gives us something to say*. Make this, and you make news. And because it's silk, you can charge ten times the price you could ever expect from the shirt you originally brought in.

Moral: Wherever possible, try to give your product or service a unique selling proposition. *Find something to say about it that no one else can say.*

HOW TO KEEP THEM READING

THE SMALL PRINT.

*"All politicians have bandanna words guaranteed to
raise a cheer: the mayor of Lynn. Massachussets
recommended motherhood, apple pie and tax relief".*
Nancy Banks Smith

CHAPTER SIX

Back in 1962, Volkswagen ran an advertisement for their VW Beetle. It broke every rule in the book. It had no picture and no slogan. It had very little text matter, and the headline held no promise. It simply said: "How to do a Volkswagen Ad". The body copy went on thus:

1. Look at the car.

2. Look harder. You'll find enough advantages to fill a lot of ads. Like the air-cooled engine, the economy, the design that never goes out of date.

3. Don't exaggerate. For instance, some people have gotten 50 m.p.g. and more from a VW. But others have only managed 28. Average: 32. Don't promise more.

4. Call a spade a spade. And a suspension a suspension. Not something like "orbital cushioning".

5. Speak to the reader. Don't shout. He can hear you. Especially if you talk sense.

6. Pencil sharp? You're on your own.

Now I'd like to point out at once, this *isn't* the kind of advertisement you can run. Or indeed, many bigger advertisers could run. You can put out that kind of publicity only if you have a history of prolonged advertising behind you, have built up a major following, and know people are familiar with the benefits of your car. And you must have literally millions to spend. To the best of my knowledge, this advertisement ran only in the USA, where they have more awareness of advertising, are used to out-of-the-ordinary approaches and are prepared (by long exposure) to laugh with certain advertisers.

But Volkswagen advertisements (and not just this example, but many) are good models on which you can base your own writing. Consider:

1. It starts with a fillip. A short pithy sentence, which is a surprise, raises a quiet smile, and yet is so obvious (once you've thought of it) it must take the reader along to the next step. It tells you simply to "Look at the car". From which you can learn the first trick in writing body copy for advertising. Don't start with the name of the product. That's boring. Don't repeat in the first sentence what you've already said in the headline. Don't be obvious and expected. Start if you can with a thought that makes the reader *smile*.

2. It talks sense. The words are conversational. They are simple and friendly. The only time they get into "advertisingese" is when they mock at the ridiculous style of writing some advertisers (and especially the writers of American car ads) use. They urge you to call a spade a spade, not something like "orbital cushioning". Don't try and "con" your audience. Treat them as intelligent human beings.

3. It doesn't repeat itself. The sentences follow on logically from one thought to the next. There's no dwelling too long, or heavily over-emphasising one benefit, to the stage when the reader gets bored. The writing is simple, but doesn't treat the reader like a simpleton. It's good advice to write up to your readers, rather than talk down to them. That way they won't get the feeling they're being preached at, or pressurised, or being deceived by sleight-of-pen. They can follow the reasoning, see it makes sense, and nod agreement.

4. The sentences are short. They don't meander. Each sentence contains sales points. When the sales points have been made, the writer puts in a full stop.

5. The paragraphs are short. And if you could see the ad, you'd notice that they have been set to a short measure. The point to learn here is that you shouldn't set out your words over a long "span of apprehension" to use the psychologist's phrase. The reading matter most of us are used to, and look at every day, is the newspaper, and newspapers have their type set in columns of between 1½ and 2 inches wide. That's the length of type most familiar to most readers. They expect type to be set that way. So although there's no need to keep text matter in quite such short lines in every piece of your literature, you should never forget that type can be set in too-long lines that tire the eye, so the reader gives up on you.

6. The paragraphs are numbered. This is a good technique, commonly used when preparing advertising copy. Each paragraph is of reasonable length, and there is space between each. What this ad has *not* done, but which you could well consider doing, is to add short sub-headings above paragraphs. Newspaper sub-editors are always putting in sub-headings. Often they consist of a single word. This is easy on the eye, and helps the reader over from the last paragraph of text to the next. Which is, of course, the secret of good copy. Write your last sentence in such a way that your reader *must* go on to the next.

7. There's nothing to argue with. Not one word of the VW copy is contentious. There is, on the contrary, an air of sweet reason about the piece. They even admit to an area of possible doubt. "Some drivers have only managed 28 m.p.g." Yes, says the reader, that's right. So now they've admitted that, I am much more willing to believe the other claims they've made.

8. It ends by telling you what to do. "Pencil sharp?" asks the writer. "You're on your own." There's no doubt what is expected of you. Go on, you're urged, get writing. And to emphasise the point still further, this advertisement has a space ruled up for the picture, with a small caption: "Picture goes here." A rule drawn under the picture-space, with the caption "Headline goes here." And three blocks of lines indicating where the small print should be, with the caption "Start copy here." The instructions couldn't be more precise.

Getting the right attitude

One of the things you might not immediately notice about the VW ad is that it's amusing. We've been entertained. It's as if the writer had asked us to take part in a kind of a game, and the whole thing is going to be fun. I'd like you, if you can, to carry that thought with you when you come to start writing your sales literature. You've got to enjoy it. After all, if you hate the time you spend writing your ads, it'll show through in the ads you write. If you're bored, how can you expect your readers *not* to be bored? On the other hand, if you feel enthusiastic, that sense of enthusiasm conveys itself to your customers. You've got to believe in the product. Bubble with conviction that you're selling something great. You see, there's no difference between selling in print and selling in person. If a salesman comes through your door looking glum and downcast, and is less than keen in the way he presents his wares, you'll be less than keen to listen to him. The same applies when you write sales messages. If you feel fired-up with the offer, your words will fire up your prospect. If you feel low and your writing gets soggy, then the reader gets soggy.

You are an advocate

To get your advertising into perspective, see yourself as "council for the defence". Imagine you are presenting the case for your product to a hard-nosed jury, who, when they come to consider their verdict, are voting as to whether or not you're going to stay in business. The jury are not antagonistic. Everybody understands that if there were no such thing as advertising we wouldn't know what was for sale. You're actually providing an information service, telling your customers this particular item is on the market, in their area, if they want it. That much is obvious. But fair-minded though the jury may be, they're also busy. They won't give you their time if you're going to bore them, or if you don't present your case in a way they can understand. So be a good counsel. Show your product or service in its best possible light. You've spent weeks preparing your brief, now present it with all the sales skill at your command. There's nothing to be ashamed of, or despondent about, in being an advocate. Cry your wares.

Start in the middle

We spent much of Chapter five working on our headline, and we now understand how important those words are. When you get down to the smaller print, never repeat in your first paragraph what the reader has already read. Some journalists have a technique for avoiding this. When they have written their report, they go back to the beginning, and strike out the first paragraph. If your headline is conveying as much as it should, your reader already has a good grasp of what you offer. No need to go over it again, now you must stimulate interest, back up the headline with additional facts, news and information.

Get heavy with the word "you"

I once worked with a man who refused to let me write any copy using the word "we". As in *"we believe this is one of the best offers you'll see this year"*. Or *"we urge you to send in this coupon today"*. Another ad-man I know hates the word "I". As in *"I'd like to introduce you to a totally new idea"*. Or *"I'm convinced this tyre is a major contribution to road safety"*. "You", said these men, is the word to use. The truth is somewhere in between. It *is* a good idea to use the word "you". I've been told there is a direct relationship between the number of times "you" is used, and the number of sales made. But I'm not going to say "we" and 'I' are out of court. If you find it convenient to use those conventions, go ahead.

Don't break the thread

Because you've spent a long time getting your benefits in order of importance, you should find you have a clear thread of reasoning running through your copy. That's good. It shows you've followed the discipline, the facts of your case are unfolding as they should, and you're unlikely to forget anything. But there are a number of stylistic tricks you can use to strengthen this thread.

You can use questions

"What do you want most from . . . (name your product category)."
"How does the product you use now compare with . . . "
"How would you like to be able to . . . (whatever your product does)."

You can use repetition

Some people prefer it for the way it removes stains.
Some because it makes colours fresh and bright.
Some for the way it restores carpet pile.
Some simply because it works out less expensive.

You can use numbered points

Here's how, with one product, you can 1. 2. 3. 4....

These link-phrases are worth their weight in gold

And of course...
More interesting still...
At the same time...
Just as important...
You already know...but...
For example...
That's only part of it...
Even so...
Not to mention...
This includes...
Because...
Naturally...
Did you realise...
Not only...
You see...
When all's said and done...
After all...
Just as...so...
It's as if...
Moreover...
There's more yet...
As we said at the start...
We couldn't end without...
Two final points...

You can repeat action words

SEE the cleaner lift out stains.
SEE the reds get redder, the blues bluer.
SEE how, without soap or foam...
SEE the spick-and-span result.

You can use verbs

We never fail to EMPTY the ashtrays,
FILL your tank to the brim,
CHECK the wipers and washers,
SHINE the windows,
TUNE the radio.

You can use a time sequence

When I first used this product...
After some months...
It's hard to remember when...
One incident stands out...
Even after all this time...
One final thought...

Adding interest

All the time you're writing, think about how to keep the readers reading. Turn a phrase in a way that makes them smile. Express an idea so you get them nodding in agreement. Most of all, tell them *what they don't know.* That's the one area where the journalist has a distinct advantage over the copywriter (his main disadvantage is that he must work at hair-raising speed to an inexorable deadline). But he does have specific news to report. You may not have news in the "it-just-happened" sense, although there's no harm in bringing a topical reference into your text. Your ammunition is the facts and figures about the product, and you might well swot up on all its aspects by dipping into an encyclopedia.

Clinching the sale

After a while you have to *convince* the reader you've got what he needs. Conviction lies in your ability to put yourself into your customer's mind, and ask the questions he would ask. Raise the doubts he has, then assuage them. You can reassure with tone of voice as well as information, by avoiding the hackneyed phrase, not over-claiming, but sounding the plain honest Joe you are. When the last shot is out of your locker, the time comes to ask for the business; that's when you tell the prospect *what you want him to do*. He can fill in the order form. He can pick up the 'phone and ask to speak to Mr (give him a name). He can call in and see you any time, at any of the offices listed below. Or he can complete and return the coupon at the bottom of the advertisement.

THE PRINCIPLES IN PRACTICE

I now want to quote from three advertisements, which demonstrate what I've been saying. The first shows a teenager lying dead in the road with his jacket draped over his face. The jacket is one of those black leather, studded jobs, with JETS emblazoned on the back, the regalia of a tear-away. We can also see the feet of a traffic cop and a couple of concerned spectators. The headline reads: *FRESH-KILLED CHICKEN*. And the text goes on:

Bravo.
Let's hear it for the winner.
That's him lying there – the dead one.
Or is he the loser?
You can't tell. Not that it matters very much.
Because in the idiot game of "chicken", winners and losers both die.
In the idiot game of "chicken", two cars speed straight for each other.
Head on.
With luck, one car steers clear in the nick of time.
Without luck, neither car steers clear.
And the winner and the loser are equally dead.
Some "game".
It took God Almighty to stop Abraham from making a blood sacrifice of his son.
What do you suppose it will take to make us stop sacrificing our children?
We who bear them in sterilised hospitals, stuff them with vitamins, educate them expensively, and then hand over the keys to the car and wait with our hearts in our mouths.
Too bad we educate them only to make a living, and not to stay alive.
Because right now – this year – car accidents kill more young people than anything else. Including war. Including cancer. Including anything.

DO YOUR OWN ADVERTISING

Riveting stuff. It goes on to urge us all to work for safer roads, and suggests a number of ways they can be made safer. The punchline is:

We at Mobil sell gasoline and oil for our living, to the living.
Naturally, we'd like young people to grow up into customers.
But for now we'd be happy if they'd simply grow up.

I've quoted this ad because I want to point out to you the "tricks" the writer used. Let's look at the piece again.

Bravo.
Short, pithy, ironic opening. Wry and unexpected, demanding that we read on.
Let's hear it for the winner.
Colloquial language. But who is the winner?
That's him lying there – the dead one.
The copy refers you back to the picture. Good technique to use.
Or is he the loser?
It's a question. We want to know the answer. Again we read on.
You can't tell. Not that it matters very much.
The secret lies in the last two words – very much. Of course it matters.
Because in the idiot game of "chicken", winners and losers both die.
Note the link-word, "because".
In the idiot game of "chicken", two cars speed straight for each other.
Note the repetition. Another technique I've mentioned.
Head on.
With luck, one car steers clear in the nick of time.
Without luck, neither car steers clear.
Repetition again.
And the winner and loser are equally dead.
Some game.
Some irony. Are you nodding?
It took God Almighty to stop Abraham making a blood sacrifice of his son.
Not Almighty God, you notice.
What do you suppose it will take to make us stop sacrificing our children?
A question.
We who bear them in sterilised hospitals, stuff them with vitamins, educate them expensively, then hand over the keys to the car and wait with our hearts in our mouths.

72

You nod agreement. This writer understands.
Too bad we educate them only to make a living and not to stay alive.
Repetition again, make a living – stay alive.
Because right now – this year – car accidents kill more young people than anything else.
That link-word "because" again. And then follows a fact we didn't know.
Including war. Including cancer. Including anything.
It's that "anything" that clinches it.

This writing looks as though it just happened, but it's an ease achieved only by effort and it uses every trick in the book, including the one of finding a subject close to the driver's heart – the subject of staying alive.

PROOF THAT "HOMEWORK" PAYS OFF

In this second example I want to prove how learning about your subject makes your work more effective. The task of the copy-writer was to persuade housewives (and, indeed, everyone who handles food) to protect it against the common housefly. A simple enough project you might think, sponsored, in this case, by HM Goverment. Think, for a moment, how *you* would tackle the job.

Now read how a top copywriter, in this case Charles Saatchi, of Saatchi & Saatchi, whose work helped the Conservative Party to defeat Labour in the 1979 election, went about the task.

His advertisement had no headline (a tactic I deplore in most advertising) but his copy was very short, and set in large type, so that in effect, the whole advertisement was a headline. It reads:

This is what happens when a fly lands on your food.
  Flies can't eat solid food, so to soften it up they vomit on it.
  Then they stamp the vomit in until it's a liquid, usually stamping in a few germs for good measure.
  Then when it's good and runny they suck it all back up again, probably dropping some excrement at the same time.
  And then, when they've finished eating, it's your turn.

And finally, in smaller print, Mr Saatchi tells the reader what to do.

Cover food. Cover eating and drinking utensils. Cover dustbins.

DO YOUR OWN ADVERTISING

Uncompromising, sharp and single-minded, this ad is made up entirely of facts. Saatchi discovered the copy, almost word for word, buried in a government-issued pamphlet on food hygiene. There's not one word of opinion, or even persuasion. And the facts, complete news to the majority of people, unroll with a horrific fascination leading to the big bad sting in the tail. The scare-mongering, justifiable in this case, is staggeringly effective. Here, in fewer than 90 words, is proof positive how, by using real information, what could have been a mundane piece of advertising became publicity that couldn't be ignored. And it's worth mentioning that the price to set the type, take the photograph and print the poster remains the same whether the writing is good or bad. The result – sales or silence – depends on work you do *before* you write the copy.

The importance of asking for the order

This last advertisement is a simple A4 leaflet, and I want to show how the writer sets out to ask for the order. His text goes like this:

Pay nothing now. Instead, accept the book on 10 days approval, completely free. So convinced are we that you'll find this an invaluable book, that we are prepared to send you a copy to study at leisure, completely without charge. You'll have time to assess its true value, and realise how useful it can be to read thoroughly, and keep by your side for constant reference. Only when you are convinced the work will benefit you, need you settle our account. Should you feel the book is not all we promise here, you simply return it within 10 days, undamaged, to our offices, and you need pay nothing.

Read, laugh, learn, and then experience the benefits you can enjoy, from John Smith's sharply observed, pithily written book.

How to get this work direct from the publisher.

1. Order on the form below. If you complete the order form now, and post it (no stamp needed) to The Gold Farthing Press, we will send you the book (or books) required by post. This will save you a trip to the shops, and a wait (if you find they have run out of copies and have to make a special order). Be sure to enclose your cheque or postal order for the correct amount.

2. Use the same order form, but request a copy on approval.

CHAPTER SIX

ORDER FORM

Clip out this form, put it in an envelope, and post it today.
Tick as appropriate.
Please send me .... copy(s) of the book. Price £20 (including package and posting) per copy.
I enclose my cheque, postal order for £... (Cheques payable to The Gold Farthing Press).
I would like the book on 10 days approval. I understand if I return it during the 10 day period I will not be charged.

Name. Job Title. Company. Address.
This order form should be mailed as soon as possible to (and here follows a name and complete FREEPOST address).

You do not need to stamp your envelope.
In case of a query please telephone (and the number).

The customer knows exactly what to do

Everything the customer needs to know, every question he might ask, is answered in this last page of the leaflet, which also carries quotes from reviews of the book, and other works by the same author. The order form gives the price of the book, who to send your cheque to and even adds a 'phone number in case of queries. The "t"'s are crossed, the "i"'s dotted, the instructions clear. The pay-off also emphasises some advantages of ordering off-the-page.

(You needn't walk to the shops. They may have run out of stock. You might have to wait. Avoid this hassle. Order here and now.)

That copywriter spent the previous three pages selling the product. Hopefully he convinced prospects the book was a good buy. It would be a pity to lose the sale at the last moment, through lack of information. The order form is big. There's plenty of space to write in. No stamp is needed (a fact stressed twice in the copy). If you're producing advertising which asks your prospect to do something, make it obvious what you want done. And make it as easy as possible for the customer to do.

WRITING THE SMALL PRINT

A CHECKLIST

1. Start with a bang
Make the reader jump. Or smile. Or be
intrigued. Don't start with the name of the
product or the name of the company.

2. Start in the middle
Don't repeat in the first paragraph what can be
seen from picture and headline.

3. Use short words and sentences

4. Have a clear train of thought

5. Be reasonable

6. Use sub-headings

7. Use facts, figures, news

8. Be enthusiastic, lively, colloquial

9. Prove your case

*10. Leave the reader in no doubt about what
to do*

C H A P T E R

14 WAYS TO ILLUSTRATE

YOUR ADVERTISING.

AND WHEN TO USE THEM.

"People believe in photography in the way they don't believe in the painted image. To them the painting is a fantasy, but the photograph somehow seems real".
David Bailey.

In truth, of course, there's no limit to the ways you can illustrate your advertising. You can use a photograph, but the photo can be of anything you like. You can use a drawing, but the drawing can be of anything you like. This chapter is intended to cover the fourteen most commonly used *techniques*, why they're used, what's good (and bad) about each, and what guidelines you can consider when deciding on a particular technique. If you look through the following pages before you read the text, you might be bewildered by the choice. There's an embarrassment of riches. However, alongside each illustration I've laid down some general outlines about when and why this particular style might suit you. Let's see how we go.

1. THE PHOTOGRAPH
This is the most commonly used, and generally the most successful way to illustrate the greater part of advertisements and sales material. Why?

People are used to looking at photographs
When you open a newspaper or magazine, the photograph predominates. It can be in colour, if the product you are selling depends on colour for its appeal. It's easy to "read". It's an accurate picture of what you're showing. It's familiar and it's well accepted.

People believe photographs
You can test this yourself. You know when you pick up a holiday brochure, most of the hotels and beaches shown are photographed. Then you come to one hotel which is drawn. Immediately you grow suspicious. Maybe the hotel isn't finished. Maybe there's a gasometer or rubbish tip behind to spoil the view. A hundred things might be wrong and the fact that the travel company hasn't photographed it, to *prove* it's OK, makes you circumspect. What's the catch? This wariness of illustrations in travel brochures (born of bitter experience) carries over into publicity. Not all publicity – there are times when an artist's version of the product can be positively beneficial. But remember photographs are authentic, credible and provide proof that your product is *like that*. You're not cheating.

You can retouch photographs
Despite all that, you might be in a situation where you get a less than perfect photograph. Perhaps there's some eyesore in the background. Perhaps part of your shot contains too much shadow which you can't

Continued on page 82

PHOTOGRAPHER'S STUDIO
50 Rushworth Street, London SE1 0RB. Telephone 071-261 9566.
(My special thanks to Roy Wales for providing the picture.)

Most advertising photographs are taken in a studio like this. It may
seem a bit big for the simple task of taking pictures, but in fact you
can re-create virtually any indoor scene in a good studio. I've seen sets
that look like rooms in the British Museum (where photography is
forbidden) and worked in huge hangars where, protected from the
weather, a photographer can take time lighting and shooting cars,
trucks and giant earth-movers. This hall is owned and run by Roy
Wales. There are changing rooms either side of the stage where models
dress and make-up. A kitchen allows for the preparation and cooking
of food, both to be eaten and photographed. You can see the two room-
sets (bedroom and dressing-room) that had been built when this picture
was taken. In common with many other photographers, Wales stocks
a variety of felts, back-drops and useful props and his stylist knows
where to find any object that isn't already on the premises.

DEVELOPING AND PRINTING
Virtually all professional photographers develop and print their own

shots. Wales does his in rooms below the studio, which also act as a base for two location photographers and where material and furnishings are stocked ready to be used as props and backgrounds for pictures in catalogues and brochures. Wales will also do close-up work (known in the trade as table-top) and take "pack-shots", that is, pictures of the product in its pack, which may appear a simple thing to photograph until you try to make it look as good as the client would like. Then you understand why some pack-shots can cost hundreds of pounds.

THE PROFESSIONAL PHOTOGRAPHER.

The Creative Handbook, which is a directory of the advertising business, lists over 600 professional photographers working in London and probably twice that many with studios in the regions. Their governing body is the Association of Photographers, which claims to establish a proper code of practice to see you are treated fairly by the photographer – and get a good, professional job – and at the same time, treat the photographer properly, not expecting him to produce the impossible, nor holding him personally responsible for what the weather might do, if you're working on location (you can insure *against* rain, or *for* sun and snow; indeed you can insure almost anything on a photographic shoot, including the model's legs).

There is no standard fee for a day's work with a professional photographer; what you pay depends on who you hire, and rates vary from around £350 a day for a good sound job, to perhaps as much as £1,700 a day if you're on some far-away location, using a photographic mega-star and working on international business. Some photographers specialise in a single subject: they'll produce mouth-watering shots of food, or make cars look twice as long as they really are, or take fashion shots, room-shots or possibly still-life. Others go to the opposite extreme and make their money in industrial photography, in factories, on building sites and in shipyards and foundries. But the further from the big cities you go, the fewer specialists you find, and the majority of professionals in the smaller towns are happy to accept any assignment.

WHY NOT BUY A PICTURE "OFF-THE-PEG"?

You may wonder whether you need to take a photograph at all, or whether one doesn't already exist of the scene you want. To find out, consult *The Creative Handbook* again, which lists photo-libraries, picture-researchers and studios which may well find the set-up you're looking for in their existing stocks. This will not mean you're buying cheap, since fees are rarely low. But it will mean you can have a picture by a top lensman (perhaps of an exotic location) without paying the travel expenses and the fares and fees of the models used. You are, of course, saving money, but the picture (or pictures) can still cost you

DO YOUR OWN ADVERTISING

£200 a time or more. There are also photo-libraries which specialise in famous personalities. Say you want to use a picture of a member of the House of Commons in your literature, or someone who is currently in the news. Provided you assume the responsibility for getting their permission to use the photograph, specialist libraries can find you terrific pictures of well-known people.

However, you should be aware of the Independent Broadcasting Authority's *Code of Advertising Standards and Practice*, paragraph 13 of which states: "Individual living persons should not normally be portrayed or referred to in advertisements without their permission. However, reference to living persons may normally be made in advertisements for books, films, radio or TV programmes, newspapers, magazines, etc., which feature the person referred to in the advertisement, provided it is not offensive or defamatory."

This rule (introduced May 1985) outlaws advertisements such as those run by the GLC and the makers of the game "Trivial Pursuits" which featured people "in the public domain" (i.e. politicians) without their prior knowledge or permission. You cannot circumvent the rule with a disclaimer such as "The use of illustration here does not indicate any endorsement by the person illustrated".

lose in the developing room. Perhaps part of the product detail has been lost, from an area that's important. Defects like these can often be rectified. You will need to find a skilled retoucher, of course, but if you tell him what you think is wrong with the picture, and give him a reference of the product to copy from, he can add detail, lose fuzzy areas, paint out spots and blotches, improve the lighting, take away the creases in a suit and so on. I don't mean you should use retouching to misrepresent your product, that simply leads to trouble. But photographs can be improved if you get an expert to do it, and improved without the reader knowing, because skilled retouching doesn't show.

Photographs are authentic

You know the phrase "the camera can't lie". Well, among this list of 14 ways is an example of where the camera has lied. Not to deceive, but to improve the way the message communicates (see the advertisement for hair colorant). There are times when your customer must have an accurate and detailed picture of what you're selling, so he knows exactly what it looks like, what the pattern is, where the knobs and indentations are. When clarity and accuracy matter, go for the photograph.

Photographs are easy to get

The world is full of advertising photographers. Some of them, like David Bailey and Patrick Lichfield, are household names, and their fees higher than most advertisers like to afford. But every town has its commercial photographers and some can be very good. Moreover, they understand advertising, and will be able to advise you on the best ways, times and places to have your shots taken. Check through *Yellow Pages*, find someone near you and ask him to bring along his portfolio (which contains examples of his work) so you can judge for yourself the kind of job he'll produce. Professional photographers have a scale of charges, so you'll know beforehand what your photographic session will cost, and whether that fee includes the price of the film used, development charges and so on.

Photographs convey scale

Most of the time your customers will know the size of the product you're selling. A teacup and saucer, a dustpan and brush, a dining table and chairs, all come in an expected size. But say you're selling model cars, statuettes or carvings, or you want to emphasise how small your product is (with the coming of miniaturisation, smallness can be a sales-point). Then you include in the picture a human hand, or a matchbox, or other article the size of which everybody knows. Or (most obvious of all) print alongside your photograph ACTUAL SIZE.

When to use the squared-up photograph

Squared-up simply means the photograph is in the shape of a box. It can be square, oblong or upright. It can stretch the length or width of the page. But if it's in a rectangular shape, it's known as squared-up. Squared-up photographs are best used in the following conditions:

* In a catalogue.

* When selling food. (Remember, we eat with our eyes.)

* When selling something unfamiliar (a new species of flower or potted plant, for example, or an exotic, imported product).

* When you want to show a *result* of something (a dress badly stained before cleaning, and perfect after).

* When you want to show your product *in situ* (readymade curtains on a window, or a new fireplace in a living room).

* When you want to convey accurately, and in detail, precisely what your product looks like.

* When eye-appeal is paramount.

When not to use the photograph

If you're selling a product, rather than a service, I believe that for most of the time the photograph will serve you well. But there are some products where it's a waste of selling power.

* Don't photograph a gramophone record. Instead show the performers, or create an "atmosphere".

* Don't use photos in *Yellow Pages*. They won't print clearly; a line drawing is better.

* Don't use photos in small spaces in your local paper. A new line in dresses can be better sold by letting an artist create the "impression". The customer can see and feel the goods when she gets to the shop.

* If your product *makes* something, photograph *what it makes*.

* Don't photograph pens, artist's brushes, pencils or markers. Show the effects they create.

* Don't photograph pastry shapers. Photograph the kinds of biscuits and tarts they produce.

* Don't photograph skeins of wool, show what you can knit with them.

2. THE CUT-OUT PHOTOGRAPH

Obviously, this begins as a box shape, but your artist or printer blocks out part of the box, so all you have left is the product, or the product with only *part* of the background. When is the cut-out photograph useful?

* When you want to show a person, but not *where* they are. (The human body, either head and shoulders or full length, cuts out rather nicely, and you can fit your typematter round the outline.)

* To ring design changes in a page of squared-up pictures.

red-up.   Cut-out.   Courtesy of Bob Bernard

* When there is an unnecessary item in the background which distracts or mars the scene.

* When you have to photograph in the winter, but your advertising appears year-round. (You cut out leafless trees, snow, etc.)

* When you want to focus attention on the product exclusively, with no other distraction or surround.

3. THE LINE ILLUSTRATION

This is a picture drawn only in black and white. It has no shading, no tones or tints, no greys. It can be as simple, complicated, or lifelike as you like. Or it can be surreal and "way-out". When is the line illustration valuable?

* When you are printing on coarse paper (as in your local newspaper).

* When you want to create atmosphere and don't mind losing a little authenticity.

85

1. Cost: £30.40 Time: 2 days

2. Cost: £42.87 Time: 1 day

3. Cost: £53.40 Time: 2½ days

4. Cost: £111 Time: 2 days

Line illustrations, courtesy of Spectron Artists

* When your illustration is very small.

* When you design a trade mark.

* When you want to illustrate something that doesn't exist.

* When you want to inject humour or style, but don't want the effect to be "cartoon-y".

here is virtually no limit to the styles in which line drawings can be lone. The thing to remember is that while they add interest, amusenent and information and can be useful when advertising in local lewspapers, you lose authenticity and believability. If it matters to our customer to *see* the product in authentic detail, think first about photograph.

Line and tone illustration
Artist: Peter Byatt
Spectron Artists

. THE LINE AND TONE ILLUSTRATION

Again, this is a "one-colour" picture, generally black against white. But as well as the lines, you have shades, tones and tints. Some tints are laid mechanically, others applied with brush, conté crayon or magic marker. The advantage is that they add dimension, and, in ome cases an almost photographic effect can be achieved. The line and tone is especially effective in high-fashion illustrations. When will t pay you to use line and tone?

* When you want realism without photography.

* When you want to exaggerate for effect.

* When you want to create atmosphere. (Black and white line and tone can help with "speed" effects, "spooky" atmosphere and humour.)

* When you want a surreal picture.

* When you're selling high fashion. (The best fashion artists can add emphasis to the "features" of a garment without making them seem over-emphasised.)

* When you want impact but not full colour.

* When you find an artist whose work hits exactly the tone you want.

This last point obviously applies to all illustrations. You may find examples of work you like in a newspaper, magazine or artist's portfolio. You can also buy an *Art Directors Index*, which is specially produced to give you a guide to the many different kinds of illustrations available.

5. LINE DRAWINGS IN COLOUR

Mickey Mouse, Donald Duck and most of the original Disney characters are line drawings in colour. The colour is flat and solid. There's no shading or grading. Which isn't to say a coloured line drawing need always be a cartoon. It could just as easily be technical. The point is, it's all *line*. When should you use it? These guidelines apply.

* Remember, it's an illustration, so won't carry photographic authenticity.

* It can add humour, deftness and a light touch.

* It can give you crazy, zany, impossible pictures.

* It can be used to emphasise.

* Generally speaking it's better used in small pictures.

6. FULL COLOUR DRAWINGS

There are as many types of full colour illustration as there are artists to create them. The main difference is in the materials used to carry out the work. They can be done in pencil and crayon, water colours, oils, magic markers or pen and ink. They can be wild, stylish, horrific, madly funny or painted with such realism they're impossible to tell from a photograph, but the more detailed and realistic they are, the more you'll have to pay. For the smaller business which doesn't have a fortune, the dramatic full colour illustration may be out. But there are things it can do even the best photography can't.

* It can make fantasy appear as reality.

* It can be so much larger than life.

* It can make even a Rolls Royce seem more attractive. (In fact car advertising is an area where a "real-life" illustration is frequently used.)

Line drawing in two colours
Artist: Bob Bernard

DO YOUR OWN ADVERTISING

Full colour fashion drawing
Artist: Donald Gott
Spectron Artists

* It can glamorise, dramatise and create emotion the way no other artwork can.
(The right artist will paint you a scene of the 21st century that makes it seem you've taken a camera into the future.)

Artist: David Edgell

7. BLACK AND WHITE CARTOONS

Easy to commission, since thousands of artists can produce them. Cheap to use, immensely useful to dot around. Here are some examples of when to use them.

* To add light relief to a sales story.

* To emphasise specific points.

* To break up long paragraphs.

* To encourage readers to turn the page.

8. CARTOONS IN FULL COLOUR

Walk into your local stationer's, take a look at the greetings card section, and you have a display of coloured cartoons. Here again there are as many styles as there are artists. Cartoons don't *have* to be funny, they can demonstrate or inform, or even be sad. Use them as follows:

* To emphasise sales points.

* To add interest to columns of text.

Cartoon in colour
Artist: David Edgell
Spectron Artists

* To demonstrate.

* To add humour.

* To encourage the eye to read on.

* To indicate any action you want the reader to take.

9. THE STRIP CARTOON

If you believe government statistics, there are nearly two million barely literate adults in the UK. The strip cartoon is a good way to reach them, and research shows strip cartoons have high attention value. Here are some good times to consider them.

* If you want to tell your story as a *sequence of events*.

* If you're advertising to children, teenagers or barely literate adults.

* If you're advertising in a children's comic. (Some comics are even prepared to reduce the cost of your advertisement – and maybe provide you with an artist – if you run your ad as a strip cartoon. It helps to make the comic seem better value, and "hides" the fact it's running advertising.)

THE STRIP CARTOON

Dan Dare was the apogée of the strip cartoon, drawn in 1950 by artist Frank Hampson, later voted the best comic-strip storyteller in the world. I've chosen this particular issue because it shows a page of story told without a word of dialogue. In 1961 Hampson disappeared into the wilderness and although mourned by a million schoolboys, never re-emerged. He died on 9th July 1985, aged 66.

Eagle reproduced by kind permission of IPC.

* When you want to be conspicuous in a page of newsprint. (You know yourself how the eye seeks out a strip cartoon.)

* When education is involved (e.g. you're demonstrating how to erect, use or dismantle your product).

10. CUT-AWAY ILLUSTRATION

This work is normally used to show the "engineering" or "technical" aspects of a subject, while at the same time letting the reader see the "outside" of the car, aircraft, tank, or whatever is being sold. The artist is generally expected to get the technical aspect of drawings like these absolutely accurate; indeed you might find yourself in legal difficulties if he does not. For this reason alone he must be allowed to work from blueprints, computer printouts, etc. and be given as much access to detail as he wants. Getting it "roughly right" will not be considered good enough; even schoolboys have been known to write in and point out errors to advertisers. Occasions when a "cut-away" is appropriate generally suggest themselves, but as well as for showing mechanical details you might like to consider:

* If you have occasion to show the inside of the human body.

* If you want to show how much quality goes into the assembly of your product.

11. THE MONTAGE

This technique is popular (indeed over-popular) with first-time advertisers, who believe they have a lot to say, and can get it all into one picture if they use a montage. It is also very common on film posters; in fact I spent a miserable half-hour with an American publicity expert (so-called) who told me that a lifetime in film advertising had taught him that every good film poster had to have a girl, a gangster and a gun. He said that after rejecting a dozen posters advertising what the distributors considered to be a "difficult" film – in other words anything that hasn't already proved itself at the Hollywood box office. Deferring to his experience I withdrew to do more work, pausing only to wonder how he'd advertise *Romeo and Juliet*. (I already knew the answer, they showed Romeo and Juliet in bed in the nude.) It's perfectly true the montage lets you get it all in, but I fear it also allows you to be lazy, and not decide what your main promise is. However, montages can be useful sometimes:

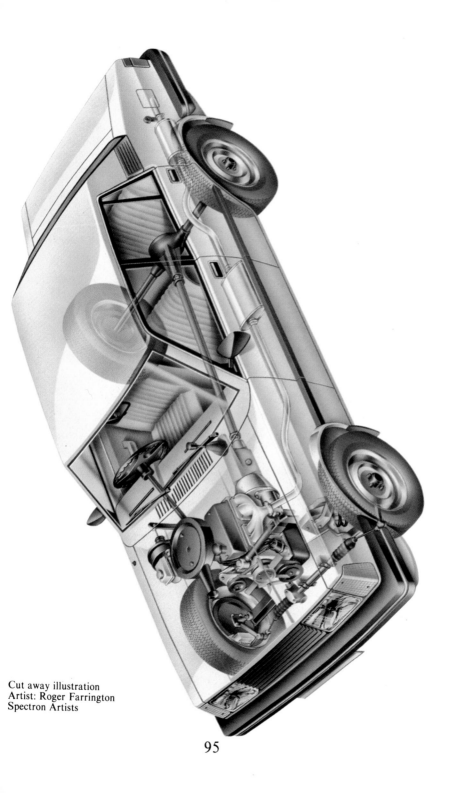

Cut away illustration
Artist: Roger Farrington
Spectron Artists

DO YOUR OWN ADVERTISING

The Montage technique
Artist: Peter Byatt
Spectron Artists

* When there really is nothing specific to emphasise, and you want your story to look busy.

* When you want to create apparent "value-for-money" and can't do it by focusing on "single" items.

* When the product genuinely *is* for "everybody". (And to be frank, I can't think of one).

NOTE: On my bookshelf are some dozen works full of examples of good advertising, from across the globe. In these books, there isn't a single advertisement which used a montage as its illustration.

12. THE TECHNICAL ILLUSTRATION

Although the example here is in black and white, you can commission technical work in colour as well. And notice, too, the numbers and arrows pointing to different parts of the car engine. This is a technique that can make technical drawing a very interesting part of your

Technical illustration, courtesy of Spectron Artists

advertisement, especially if you set a "key" by the side (or beneath) naming the numbered parts. This kind of work can be used for technical publications but need not be confined to them; indeed if you want to impress the layman with the quality of your goods, a technical drawing helps to do that. When you go to engineers, however, please be sure to get it right, or be ready to answer the carping that will arrive in your mail. Use this work when:

* You want to show a technical aspect in a brochure of photographs.

* You want to ring changes in the design of your page.

* You want to highlight a particular point you consider is key to clinching a sale. It might, for instance, be the part of your product which only your company makes in this special way.

* You want to direct attention to a number of areas in a confined space (the numbers and arrows are the secret here).

* You want to set up a puzzle, as the advertiser did here.

13. ARCHITECTURAL DRAWING

The main reason for this kind of work is that your illustrations have to be technically acceptable and accurate to the profession you're talking to. You can imagine a brochure commending yourself as an expert at extending houses, which is dropped through the door of an architect who proceeds to tear it to pieces because the illustration is wrong!

I don't recommend that you prepare this kind of work often, since it is expensive and you'll need a specialist to produce it. Rather, it is included here to remind you of the breadth of illustrations that are available to the advertiser. But occasions where it can help are:

* When it is important to show technical expertise.

* When you are showing specific examples of work done.

* When your qualifications and ability must be demonstrated.

* When your audience is highly sophisticated.

* When you're producing actual recommendations rather than advertising material.

Courtesey of John Gill Associates
Architects and Planning Consultants

* When you're submitting material for publication in your technical or trade press. (For example, in a feature article.)

14. TRICK PHOTOGRAPHY

Say you make a range of nine different hair colorants, and you want to show them all in one advertisement. Overleaf you'll see how a New York advertising agency did it for their clients, Clairol Inc., in 1961. You're not looking at a model, instead you're looking at a mirror, cut into 2″ strips and glued to a board. The board is then bent towards you with the model looking into it. Somehow, the photographer manages to get her without letting the camera be seen; don't ask me how they managed it, ask Jerry Schatzberg (the lensman) and Bert Steinhauser (the inventive art director from the agency). Trick photography is too glib a way to describe this kind of professionalism, which allowed the agency to take one photograph (instead of nine) and colour in the hair later, to give an exact match to each of the tones Clairol had to offer.

I've included this advertisement not because you can steal the idea (the copyright belongs to Clairol Inc. USA, all rights are reserved

EXTRA-LITE A* WHITE BEIGE SILVER BEIGE* EXTRA-LITE PLATINUM MOONBEAM BLONDE* IVORY CHIFFON* 24 TOWHEAD* NUDE BEIGE* CHAMPAGNE BEIGE*

NOW BE ANY OF THESE DELICATE BLONDES!

Close your eyes for a moment and pretend your hair is as pale and romantic as Ivory Chiffon . . . or Champagne Beige . . . or any heavenly blonde shade you've ever dreamed of. It's a beautiful daydream. Make it come true . . . with Clairol's Creme Toner, the only color cosmetic that creates this range of 22 pale, *delicate* blondes!

First your hair needs Ultra-Blue* Lady Clairol* Lightener. Then select the shade of blonde you want to be. Clairol's Creme Toner does the rest. (It works gently . . . and it leaves your hair *feeling* like silk.) Your hairdresser loves Clairol's Creme Toner . . . and you'll love living your life as a blonde. CLAIROL* CREME TONER*

Creme Toner is a Trademark of Clairol Inc. for its Oil Shampoo Tint. *Trademarks © 1963 Clairol Inc., Stamford, Conn. Also available in Canada.

and the picture has been printed by permission of the copyright holders) but to alert you to the fact that by using imagination, photography can help to solve selling problems. An ordinary advertiser would have shown the girl with one type of hair colorant and either printed colour-swatches at the base of the advertisement or shown the nine packs. Or, in cases where the agency is especially lazy, simply listed the other eight colours. When you come to thinking about photographs, if you have a range of colours to show, consult your photographer about the best way to show them. Take this book with you, and show him how Clairol did it. He'll be fascinated by the shot and inspired to come up with an approach that will help you.

WHO'RE YOU TRYING TO IMPRESS?

A famous Hollywood tycoon was looking for a UK ad-agency to promote his films. To try them out, he gave them a tiny sum of money and asked them to demonstrate how good a job they could do advertising one London-shown movie.

There are a lot of ways they could have spent the cash. Maybe with trailers on Thames TV. Maybe with spaces in a London evening paper. Maybe with small classified ads in the Entertainment columns. Maybe with bus-sides on London Transport. Maybe with radio commercials on Capitol and LBC. What worried the agency was that the tycoon was flying over to judge their efforts.

He would be met at Heathrow and driven to the city by chauffeured Rolls. What the agency did was to snap up a couple of big poster sites inside the arrivals lounge at the airport. Another at the airport exit. More along the route to his hotel. And the last, as near to Grosvenor House (where he was staying) as possible.

Almost as soon as he left Customs, the publicity hit him. All the way to town dramatic advertising exhorted the Brits not to miss this great film. And all done on a shoestring. Certainly an ad agency who could get this kind of coverage for peanuts deserved more of his business. If the tycoon couldn't turn his head without seeing his own advertising, how well must Londoners be informed?

C H A P T E R

8

STEP-BY-STEP THROUGH AN
EIGHT-PAGE BROCHURE.

"I have yet to see any problem, however complicated, which, when you looked at it in the right way, did not become still more complicated."

Paul Anderson

CHAPTER EIGHT

I can't, in this chapter, devise exactly the brochure for you. You have your own product and your own promise. Short of coming round to meet you, and getting to know your sales problem, all I can do is set down guidelines. But if you've never prepared sales literature before, or if you've done it but felt you were groping in the dark, this chapter should keep you on the right lines. The first thing is to set down your company's needs; do this by asking the following :

* What is the purpose of your brochure?

* Who do you want to talk to?

* How will you distribute it?

* What size should it be?

* How many pages do you need?

* How many colours do you need?

Don't start to write or draw anything until you know the answers. Homework – as I keep saying – is vital. It's the fertiliser in which your ideas and words grow. Let's look at the questions more closely.

What is the purpose of your brochure?

You could want it to cold canvass, where the customer knows nothing about your company, isn't expecting any literature and may not be remotely interested in what you sell. The cold canvass is to gather leads to see whether it's worth taking your sales effort further, either with more literature, or a visit from your rep. Don't cold-call with a lavish, expensive brochure. It should be cheap to produce and distribute, telling about yourself, that you're in the market, and inviting enquiries.

Don't produce a costly brochure to drum up enquiries.

The leaflet in response to an enquiry

This is quite different. Your customer has expressed an interest in your product, and you have a real opportunity to sell. If you're creating literature in answer to a coupon reply, a telephone enquiry or letter, give it all you've got. Leads are valuable. They cost a lot to find. When one arrives don't let it go. I once spent my weekends working in a shop. Every time a customer came in, there was a chance to sell. I got the shock of my life when, the first time I let someone walk out without

105

buying anything, the boss came out from his cubbyhole and tore me off a strip. When I explained we didn't have what the customer wanted, he told me to offer something else. Get out a number of lines, talk about them, demonstrate the advantages, suggest alternatives, tell her there's something better on the market, think about her problem and find a different way to solve it. "Never let anyone walk out without buying *something.*" Later I realised he wasn't totally callous, and his strictures were to an innocent on his first day at work. But the principle is clear.

If you're preparing brochures to send in reply to a specific enquiry, sell for all you're worth.

Literature for your showroom

This is different again. You've got the customer in the salesroom asking about a particular product or service. If you offer a number of services, it can be good policy to have leaflets explaining each. Not because you might make a sale on that occasion, but because you want to publicise the different aspects of your business.

Literature for display in store needn't be lavish or lengthy. Just factual.

So before you set down to write your leaflet, make up your mind which of these purposes you're doing it for.

Who are you talking to?

This gives you a guide to the tone of voice you'll talk in, and the substance of what you want to say. Is your prospect a man or a woman? Are they well-to-do or earning less than average? Is the purchase a major decision or is it an impulse decision? I have emphasised already how important it is to *know* your customer. The better idea you have of who you're selling to, the better case you can prepare. Ask yourself also whether the reader of the material is the one who makes the purchase decision, and whether the wife will discuss it with the husband or vice-versa. If discussion is likely include reasons why the purchase is of benefit to *both.*

How is your brochure distributed?

Is it a handbill, to be stuffed through letter boxes? Then make it cheap and cheerful. Is it part of a direct-mail campaign? Then it should be comprehensive, detailed and persuasive, and cost the least it needs to, without making it tatty. Is it being inserted into a magazine? Be sure to check the maximum size the magazine(s) you're going to use will accept. And *read* the magazines before you use them. It gives you a better idea who your customers are.

What size should your brochure be?

It depends on how much you have to say. But *stick to the standard paper sizes*. A4 is the most common. A5 is also useful. Don't go for irregular sizes, even if someone tries to sell you one. It's a waste of money because to get a brochure in an irregular size, you'll have to trim off the standard-size sheet. The part you cut off you still have to pay for. So unless there is an overpowering reason to be different, don't be.

A note about "A" sizes

The "A" series system of sizing paper was first adopted in 1922 in Germany, where it is still referred to as DIN A. The sizes are calculated in such a way that each size is made by dividing the size above into two equal parts. The sizes are all the same geometrically, as they are made using the same diagonal. The basic size is AO – which is one square metre in area. You should remember that the A series sizes refer to the *trimmed* sheet; the untrimmed sizes are known as RA. About 26 countries have officially adopted the "A" system, and this can matter if you're preparing literature for abroad. By sticking to an "A" size, you know that your material will fit into the reference file of an overseas customer.

How many pages?

The *usual* number of pages most companies most frequently need, are as follows:

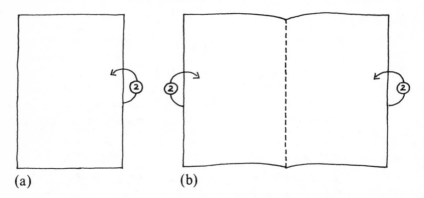

(a)   (b)

(a)   One sheet of paper. That's two sides. You can print on one or both. I recommend both. After all, you've paid for the reverse side, use it.

(b)   An A3 sheet, folded once. That gives you four sides of A4, quite enough to do a good selling job.

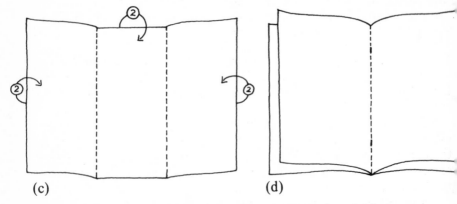

(c)   (d)

(c)   If you want a six-page leaflet, you'll need to fold the paper twice. This is called a "roll-fold".

(d)   Two A3 sheets, folded and stapled in the centre. That gives you eight A4 sides, and will make a substantial brochure.

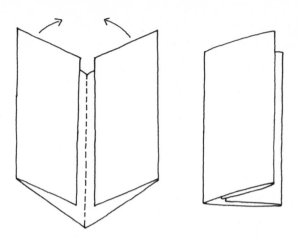

An alternative way to use eight pages is a "gate-fold". The advantage of this way of folding is that you end up, when the leaflet is fully opened out, with a four-page spread.

The thumbnail sketches explain all.

How many colours?

I suggest the following: I think a one-colour leaflet is dull and looks cheap. If you go for one colour, chose black. It's the colour everyone is used to reading, and black type on white paper is the most easily read.

I like two-colour leaflets, which are black and one other colour. In effect this gives you three colours, because you can use the colour of the paper as your third. Moreover, if you use tints and tones, you can create a pleasantly varied effect, so your reader is unaware that you've used only two colours.

Three colours are a waste of time. You can – as I've said – create three-colour effects using only two inks. If you run three inks your costs are likely to be as high as if you run four, and if you run four you've got FULL colour. In other words, yellow, red, blue and black will reproduce all the colours of the spectrum.

When to use four colours

Two general rules:

1. Is colour a sales feature of your product?

There are some instances where, quite clearly, it is. If you're selling furniture or fabrics, food, paints, wallpapers, crayons, stationery, any product where your customer will choose *depending* on colour, print your material in *full* colour. If you can't afford colour on every page, use it on some. In an eight-page brochure, it's easy and practical to produce some pages in colour. I'd plump for the outside, or centre pages. Put most of your illustrations on the full-colour pages and most of your type matter on the others.

2. Is your purpose to create "prestige"?

There are times when a company isn't selling anything much, but wants to boost its image and prestige. Company reports are a case in point. The practice here is to use full colour, since it implies the company is successful and prosperous, and can afford "expensive" literature. Colour increases readership, and helps create atmosphere. If that is part of your intention, opt for colour.

When to avoid colour

If your product or service doesn't *depend* on colour for sales appeal, why use it? Animal foods, for instance, are generally an unattractive colour; what matters is how nutritious they are, how they arrive on the farm, how easy they are to store and distribute, and so on. *Colour is less likely to matter if you're selling a service.* But apply common-sense, and talk to colleagues and sales people. They might convince you colour matters, and that the company should bear the extra expense. Certainly it helps to create "image" and increase readership. If in doubt, check out with your local printer what your brochure will cost to print in one or two colours, compared to what you'll pay for full-colour. When everything is taken into consideration, the right decision will emerge.

THROUGH THE BROCHURE STEP BY STEP

I now want to take an imaginary eight-page brochure, and go through the pages one or two at a time. As I said before, it's impossible to be absolutely specific, since I don't know your company or product. But I think you'll find the suggestions apply pretty much in most circumstances.

The front cover

Or how to say: "We've got something for you". The way I see it, the
front cover of any brochure has only two purposes. The first, and far
and away the most important, is to make it incontestably clear WHAT
YOU ARE SELLING. And the second is to make your offer in such
a way that the prospect TURNS THE PAGE. There are some people
who would add a third requirement, which is to introduce the company.
This is a good idea but not, in my view, sacrosanct. It's both easy and
natural to display the brand name once your reader has, so to speak,
"come inside". So include it up front if it's natural to do so, but not
if your writing becomes contrived.

How do you make it clear what you're selling; how do you *express*
the message? Simple: you SHOW and TELL. You show an illustration
of your product in its best possible light. And you say what it is,
bearing in mind always that you're expressing a promise. There is a
tendency – practised even by professional copywriters – to use the
front page as a "teaser" and to play with puns, or set up some kind
of intrigue in the hope that the reader can't resist knowing the

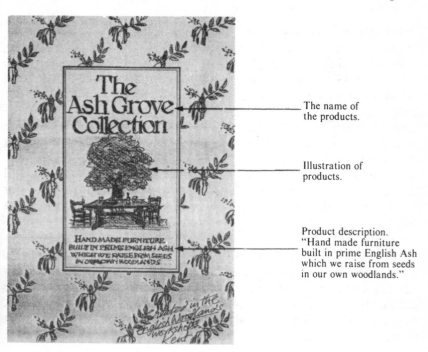

The name of
the products.

Illustration of
products.

Product description.
"Hand made furniture
built in prime English Ash
which we raise from seeds
in our own woodlands."

"answer". It's much safer, in my view, to make your offer clear, bright, enticing, and *use your picture* for all it's worth. A big, attractive picture *of the goods*, looking irresistible, is a powerful selling tool. If you're saying and showing the right things, you don't need any more "intrigue".

Pages two and three

This is where you *explain* your promise. What's in your offer for the customers. How and why they benefit. Get it all in, powerfully and clearly. It takes clear thinking to hone down your headline to precisely the right offer. The second and third pages are *not* the place to go into product detail, or show the various models and sizes you have to offer. No doubt your company makes a number of different pieces of furniture (for example) but the first spread is not the place to display them. And don't talk about the sales points of one particular item (a chair, say), talk about the advantages of owning *any* great new piece of furniture, how it enhances appearance, brings warmth, luxury and new colour to the home, yet needs a minimum of care and won't break

the bank to buy. That way the sales story for your *range* of products can be told. You get down to details when it comes to showing specific styles. That's for later on. Pages two and three are where you tell the *overall* sales story.

A good point to remember is to make these pages look like a *spread*. Do that by running your headline across both pages, and having your pictures so they "read" across both pages. I do feel if you treat the spread as a spread, and not as separate pages (in other words one page with a picture, the other with words) then you'll generally achieve more impact. One last thought on pages two and three. Encourage readers to turn over. Use an arrow, or a line saying "For more about these beautiful items turn the page", or "Six great ideas in furnishing overleaf".

Pages four and five

This is where you get down to specifics. Having made your overall pitch, begin to show the *choice and variety*. Maybe you can divide the styles by period. Maybe you divide the story up by price: "everything on this page at under £800". If you can hit on a *theme* to make the story

Welcome these pieces into your home for a 21 day trial period, without charge or obligation~

The AshGrove Collection

more easy to assimilate, do so. Order in layout indicates order in your own thinking, and means you're presenting your story simply.

Pages four and five are for quoting dimensions, naming colours and sizes, indicating subtle variations in style, generally indicating the breadth and variety of choice. *They are not the place to quote prices.* I wouldn't put prices into your brochure at all; instead have them run off separately (and cheaply). Costs and inflation being what they are, prices are almost certain to change before you run out of brochures, and you don't want to print new copies (and dump unused ones) just because your prices are out of date.

Heighten the interest

Most of pages four and five will contain large pictures of each product. But try to get variety into the design. Get photos of *detail* about a particular feature. Or emphasise the craftsmanship used to build each item. This can be done with diagrams, line drawings, or smaller (and perhaps cut-out) photos. And when you write text, be specific. Use facts, figures, and name materials. Dot your typematter with little cross-headings, make it clear which captions apply to which items (see left, see right). Better to say a lot – provided it's not repetitious – rather than leave your reader with questions unanswered.

Pages six and seven

If we've got it right so far, we've explained what our offer is, and what's in it for the buyer, and we've shown the choice available. That is, we've attracted attention, created interest and a desire to buy. What remains? First, to convince that of all the different makers or suppliers, *you're* the one to buy from. How do you do that? Start to anticipate doubts and answer questions. Are your products guaranteed? Of course, for materials, workmanship, and everything else. What other assurances can you offer? Obviously if installation is involved, you'll arrange it, and your workmen are more than experts, they won't leave until they've been round with a dustpan and brush, sweeping up every last sliver of wood, bit of plaster, nay, every speck of dust. Every installation is the personal responsibility of a company director. If customers have a problem, they can call him direct, this is the number and he'll answer after three rings.

Also tell customers how they can save money if they buy within 28 days. There's no better way to encourage a decision than to put a time limit on your offer, and suggest that after a certain date the prices will go up, or such and such a feature will be excluded from the price, or maybe, since the line is so popular, stocks will have run out.

And what about testimonials from existing customers? They're powerful and convincing. Get quotes from householders who've already bought the product, and been delighted with the speed, cleanliness and friendliness with which it was installed. A recommendation from someone independent of the company is worth more than words from the company itself. After all, nobody *has* to write a "thank-you" letter, so if they do they must have experienced service that is out of the ordinary.

Have you installed your goods anywhere special, say the Golf or Yacht Club? Page six or seven is the place to show it, with a letter from the secretary saying how the members couldn't be more pleased. If you haven't got a product in the Yacht or Golf Club, maybe you've got a contract with the local council or police force, anyone with authority, who is prepared to speak for you.

It may be your product is expensive; offer the customer a number of ways to pay. Easy terms, or credit card: install now, nothing to pay

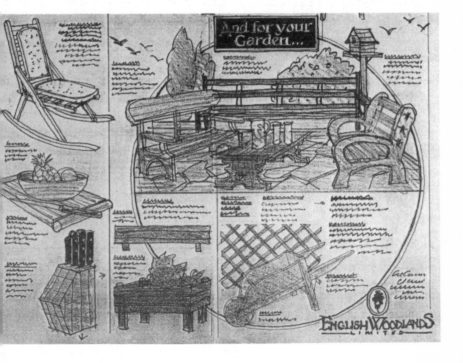

for six months! Perhaps they need to borrow? No problem – the company can recommend a respected financier connected with one of the big four banks.

And finally, tell your readers how someone comes round at the end of the day to see how the job has been done. What if the product goes wrong? Instant repair and after-sales service. Money back? Madam, we'd rather not have your money than have a dissatisfied customer to bad-mouth us. Pages six and seven are where you come up with assurances and banish doubts.

Page eight, the back cover

If you've followed the system, and made out a list of benefits, here's where the remaining items come into their own. They could include:

* Details of your showrooms. Show a map of how to get to them, and give each address and phone number.

* Space where the customer can fill in their name and address, clip out the coupon and return it to you.

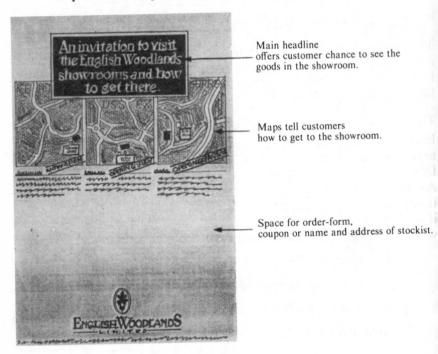

Main headline offers customer chance to see the goods in the showroom.

Maps tell customers how to get to the showroom.

Space for order-form, coupon or name and address of stockist.

This is ideal to give to a rep to make a follow-up call, or to store in your computer, so you can send out other mailings.

* A customer hot-line. You print the number boldly, give the name of someone to speak to, and reassure customers that the hot-line is open, even after hours. Messages left on tape will be attended to first thing the next day.

* State which credit cards you accept.

* Remind the reader that any special offer you've made is open for a limited period.

* Give the full address and telephone number of your head office.

* If you're talking to business people, include your fax number.

* Display the company name.

* Include your trade mark if you have one.

* Include any professional organisations you belong to.

* Include Design Centre and other awards.

The last page is also where you tell *what you want the customer to do*. Do they telephone you, ask for more information, request someone to call, come to your showroom, or fill in the order form? Whatever the action leave them in no doubt about it.

The concluding slogan

Every company likes to have a slogan, and the back page is where most brochures carry it. Well-known slogans can also be used for the front page. If you've used one there, never mind, repeat it on the back. As the old advertising adage goes: repetition is reputation. But what if you've not got one, and want to try your hand at writing it? Fine, if you've got the patience and enthusiasm. One popular way to go is what I call the "best" route. For instance:

* **For the best in hand-built furniture.**

* **The best name in hand-built furniture.**

* **The best England's cabinet-makers can build.**

* **Choose the best. Choose the Ash-Grove Collection.**

117

* **You'll feel more comfortable with the Ash-Grove Collection.**

* **The Ash-Grove Collection. Every one a collector's piece.**

* **Ash as only English craftsmen can shape it.**

* **The Ash-Grove Collection. A cut above the rest.**

To be blunt, these are so banal I'd rather not bother than include anything like that. The truth is, slogans are over-rated, and in the advertising game they pop in and out of fashion. For five years everyone has one, for the next five nobody has one and they run a different line at the bottom of every advertisement. But if a slogan is dear to your heart, I offer two pieces of advice.

1. **Make it a summary of what you offer.**

2. **Try to base it on a fact.**

The funny thing about facts and slogans is that if you use a fact, it takes you away from cliché-land. Let's try a few for our furniture company, based on facts.

* **The Ash-Grove Collection. Hand-raised, all the way from the seed.**

* **From an English Woodland, for an English home.**

* **From the furniture-makers who grow their own trees.**

* **Traditional furniture in solid English Ash.**

* **Grown, felled, matured then hand-made and polished entirely by English Woodlands.**

* **Its what happens when forester and cabinet-maker work in harmony.**

When you build a fact into your slogan it becomes more interesting and sells harder. It also tends to be something only your company can say. The truth about the product is always better than creating in a vacuum. To sum up: a brochure about your product is nothing more than the truth well told.

FREE ADVERTISING (well, almost)

Believe it or not, there are a number of places your company can advertise which cost next to nothing and which may not have occurred to you. Ask yourself the following questions, and see if you are making full use of the media you have at your disposal, today.

1. Do you use your company stationery to full effect?
A well-designed letter heading, which includes an attractive trade mark and an appropriate tag-line (slogan) is an effective way of establishing a company's image. And it can be repeated on your envelopes, on postmarks, (franking machines will even allow you to change the message from time to time), and on invoices and compliments slips.

2. Do you advertise on company transport?
Vans and trucks often have unused space on the doors and sides where you can feature the company name and a message about the business.

3. Do you use company buildings?
You've probably got the name over the door. But is it prominently displayed on the wall of your building? If you face a main road or back on to a railway line, have you a poster up there with your sales message?

4. Do you use company cars?
Provided it doesn't offend the people who use the cars, you can use tasteful branding or window-stickers to promote yourself.

5. What about calling cards?
Do they carry the company trade mark? Do they make your company look prosperous and successful?

6. Do you use meeting rooms to full effect?
You're almost certain to have one room (at least) where you meet and talk with customers and other visitors. Use the walls to display your products and other company publicity material.

7. Even your telephone answering machine can sell
A number of cinemas, leisure-centres, swimming pools and so on use recording machines to give opening times, programmes showing and to advise customers about special events. You might use yours to announce holiday dates, new telephone numbers, changes of address, or to give a number to call for personal attention, when no-one is available on that line.

C H A P T E R

ELEVEN TESTED

ADVERTISING TECHNIQUES

THAT WILL WIN YOU MORE

SALES.

"There are no new ideas in advertising."
Ed McCabe, U.S. Agency Boss

"In the whole of the literary world there are only six basic plots."
Anon.

"Everyone takes a portrait inside their heads, fifty times a day."
David Bailey

CHAPTER NINE

Unless you've slogged your way through a few advertising agencies you could be forgiven for wondering how professional copywriters produce ideas to order. When I began in the business I didn't know either, then one day I saw a seminar, advertised in our trade press, titled "New Ideas in Advertising". This was it, the secret of the universe revealed. My agency forked out the required fee and, ears pinned back, I went to listen to one of the most successful agency owner-writers in the USA. A burst of applause greeted him as he walked to the rostrum, he smiled a greeting in reply, and began thus: "Ladies and Gentlemen, my fellow creative people" – pause for effect – "there are no new ideas in advertising!" But there are a number of tried and tested techniques, which have been proven over the years to attract attention, create interest, and generate sales. I'd like to let you in on some of them.

But first – a few provisos

The following ways to make advertising can't be applied to every product or service, every time, but whatever business you're in you'll almost certainly find one or two techniques that'll prove useful. You see, while it's true there are no new ideas, what happens is writers in the ad-agencies learn how to ring changes on the old ideas, so by the time advertisements get into the newspapers or on to the screen, they *look* new. Many of the formats have been stolen from newspaper and magazine editors, who, if they can't make people read, lose their jobs. Don't be too proud to pinch a good idea if you see one – the trick is to switch it round so no one can tell. Unless they know *how* to tell, which most good copywriters do. I've picked out eleven techniques which will help companies working on modest budgets. You'll recognise them as we go.

1. The Before-and-After Technique

To use this format get *two photographs*, one of the subject before it came into contact with your company, and one after. The improvement provides the reader with proof your product or service really works. You know the kind of thing I mean. Picture A is Mr Smith who's bald on the crown of his head. That patch adds years, and takes away sex appeal. Picture B is Mr Smith after sessions with a hair clinic. Golly he's handsome, and years have fallen away. Now he can get that girl, new job, new contract or whatever, which previously baldness denied him. It is important to show *photographs* of Mr Smith since everybody believes these are genuine, whereas drawings – well, anyone can do those. I've sometimes suspected that what's happened is they found a photo of Mr Smith before he went bald, and took the second as he looks today, and switched them round. But please don't think I'm mocking. You might believe before-and-after is so simple an idea nobody can be convinced. Not so – it works for product after product, time after time.

* Curtains before dry cleaning. Dirty, stained, full of cigarette smoke, dingy and dull. Curtains after. Bright new colours, not a stain in sight, smelling of roses.

* The house before replacement windows. Dilapidated, slummy, looks like a poor residence in a poor area. The house after (when it's probably been re-painted). Worth more on the property market, draught-free, smarter and looking years younger.

* The hearth before it had a new fireplace. Boarded-up, barren, uninviting, still showing where the surround has been papered over. The hearth after, with marble and brass surround, burns bright, the room glows, the family basks.

Two other points: you can, if you like, show the "before" picture quite small and unobtrusive, and the "after" picture big and bold. But you must be sure your audience can *see* the difference. Second point, give dates, times, places, facts and figures when you caption the pictures (a caption is the small print under the picture – not to be confused with the headline, which is the big print across the top of the page). For instance, if you were selling replacement windows, under the "before" picture is: *Semi in Surbiton owned by Mr & Mrs Leslie Lucky. Sills rotting, frames rusty, panes cracked.* And beneath the "after" photo: *Two days later. Draughtproof, thief-resistant glass with non-rust aluminium frames. And the Luckys had two years to pay.*

These captions, which should be carefully positioned (for God's sake don't let your printer get them the wrong way round) say things the reader *can't see* from the shots themselves. That's the tip when you write captions. Allow the reader to study the scene and then tell him additional facts to complete the story. No point in saying: "Regency Bay leaded windows" when it's obvious they can't be anything else.

If your product or service provides a visible improvement, which you can demonstrate easily and cheaply, then before-and-after is for you. Treat it seriously, quote a testimonial from the customers saying how delighted they were and how quick, simple and inexpensive the job was. If you do it right, in a two- or three-cornered fight, chances are your *visible proof* will win the business.

2. The Comparison Technique

Comparisons, the saying goes, are odious. Sorry, but in advertising, comparisons are excellent. There's no better advice I can give than to say, if you have a better product, prove it. And there's no plainer way to prove it than to compare it with your nearest rival. You set out the benefits and advantages you offer, alongside those he offers, and show, by cross-checking, that you offer more. The great advantage about comparison advertising is that you can compare virtually anything. You can compare performance figures, and show that your product works more quickly, more thoroughly, or for longer. You can compare the materials with which you make your product, and show that because you use better materials to start with, you offer a better result. You can compare the number of times you inspect your product with the number of times your rivals inspect theirs. Or you can compare how a 20-year-old item remained perfect when treated with one substance, as opposed to a similar item which deteriorated.

You can compare the price anything costs to buy, the price it costs to run – over any length of time you choose – the price it will bring if you sell it again and the price it will cost to repair or replace. You can compare maintenance costs, time needed to service, or the skill of the men you have to employ to put it right. So much for product, price and performance.

You want to recruit someone? Use the comparison technique. It was never done better than by the Metropolitan Police, who proved that bobbies led more exciting, varied and responsible lives than your average man. The advertisements they ran asked: *"How does a week in your job compare with a week in ours?"* All you ask is: *"How does your present job compare with what we offer you at John's Company?"* Or, put another way: *"Does the job you do now offer all this?"* I ought to mention here, some companies object to comparison advertising, saying it is underhand, "knocks" the opposition unnecessarily, and – worst of all – allows them free publicity if you actually name the rival you're comparing your product against. It's neither fair nor

125

decent (they say) to pick out some poor, unsuspecting competitor, who has done your company no harm (except pinch customers) and do him down in public. Well, it's a point of view, and if you feel squeamish about the full-frontal attack, don't make it. Those who object to such determined advertising, however, cannot deny that – provided you *have* a superior product – direct comparison advertising is virtually invincible.

Moreover, there's no need to give your rival free publicity. You can still do a form of comparison advertising, without comparing your product against anything but the product your customer currently uses. You can say: "Does the toothbrush you use now have all these features?" Then go ahead and list the features, and how they help keep teeth perfect, without naming a competitor's toothbrush at all. You can even say: "No other toothbrush offers more features than the GNASHER". And once again, list the features. The "weasel" in this headline is that there may be twenty other toothbrushes which offer *just as many* features. All you've claimed is that none offers more. I used this claim when I wrote a campaign for Ryvita Crispbread, saying: "No crispbread has fewer calories". So watch the way you make your claim. If you offer only parity with rivals, then say: "Nobody offers more". But if you have a specific advantage, say: "Nobody offers as much". My own view can be summed up thus: provided you compare like with like, avoid misleading your audience and don't draw conclusions that can't be justified, it is nothing more than good salesmanship and common-sense to do comparison advertising. After all, comparing the products available to him is what every sensible customer should do before buying anything. Here are a few comparison headlines which you might be able to twist, to make them apply to your product or service.

* **Does your glue stick as many objects as our glue?**

* **How close can our hair stylists get to Vidal Sassoon's?**
  (And you show two photographs, one from Vidal's salon, the other from your own, showing that the heads have been cut and styled identically.)

* **Our suits are better than the best suit you own. Yes? No? Maybe?**
  (The yes, no, maybe, lets you off the hook and allows you to point out all the features of your suit, so the customer can judge for himself.)

* **Is your dining table crafted with as much skill as ours?**

  (And you show details again, suggesting the world's best cabinet-makers can't understand how you can offer all this skill and quality at such a reasonable price.)

* **Six ways to recognise great tailoring.**

  (And you pick out six features of your suit, suggesting they're used – as they probably will be – even by top Savile Row tailors.)

Comparison advertising provides a *format* round which to build your copy. It allows you to list, and illustrate, all your benefits. It generally makes interesting reading and shows you up in an excellent light alongside the competition. It's a tried and proven technique, encourages readership, is entirely convincing, looks transparently honest, and provides readers with the information they want! Your reps will probably use it when they speak to customers direct, if only because the customer challenges the rep with things rival products do that his product can't. Comparison advertising is an excellent promotional technique.

3. The Torture Test

So that you understand what I mean, let me give you a few examples of the torture test, which have been used in large-scale advertising campaigns. To prove a Volvo would start first time, even in deep mid-winter, the ad-agency froze the car in a block of ice, and left it for days in a deep freeze. Then they called up the AA, and had them come down to watch the car being unfrozen. When the driver's side door was sufficiently clear of ice to open, the AA inspector was given the ignition key, and invited to start the vehicle. It started first time, and the AA man said he was willing to confirm so in the advertising. This is a perfect example of a torture test, complete with an *independent authority standing by to verify he saw the test take place.*

Other torture tests I've seen used over the years include a waterproof watch being swirled around in a washing machine, and a climber wearing an anorak at the top of the Eiger, claiming the only shiver he feels is the one of excitement down his spine. Then there was the famous "sink-the-sink" test, where a manufacturer dropped a kitchen sink into the Thames for a time, hauled it out again, and showed how it came up shining, using Brand X scouring powder. A manufacturer of car locks hired a professional thief to try and break into a vehicle without being detected by the alarm. A maker of car batteries parked two cars at the North Pole. The first car had his battery installed, the second car a rival product. The test began with a driver trying to start the car with the rival battery. And naturally the engine coughs, splutters, but fails to turn over. Then we see the car with our battery installed, and – roar – the car crunches away across the ice. (If you want proof that there are no new ideas, witness the similarity between that torture test and the one for Volvo.)

The torture test is a device to prove your product really works. Torture tests are easy to dream up; just think of a situation where your product or service will be put under severe strain, and use it to demonstrate how what you sell stands up. You've proved your case, convinced your audience your goods work, even under the most unhelpful conditions, and so you can imply that in everyday life, performance is guaranteed. Torture tests also have the advantage of being interesting in themselves, since they add interest to the sales point you want to make. We call the torture test "borrowed-interest". In other words, you've devised a scenario which will demonstrate the product in action under extraordinary stress. That stress makes your story interesting. The interest is "borrowed", but it's none the worse for that, because *the hero of the story is the product.*

Now let's say you offer a catering service for the directors of large companies. The torture test could be inviting some famous chef to taste and approve (or disapprove) of the grub. If you sell dry cleaning, show how you brought a man's suit up good as new, after he wore it down a coal mine. If you run a home-gardening service, set your men to work on a derelict site (the way they worked in Liverpool to produce a dream landscape out of old docklands). The moral is clear; if you can make a rubbish-tip look wonderful, then an over-run garden presents no problems. If you run a car-repair service, rescue a model-T Ford (or other old and decrepit car), bring it back to life and display it in your forecourt, with a series of pictures showing how it was transformed. It's fascinating stuff to study, and will convince customers you know your trade. In fact you don't even need a veteran car, you can show how you repaired a smashed vehicle, made it look like new, then add a testimonial *from the owner* about how he continued to drive for another 100,000 miles with nothing more than attention at service intervals.

I think I've said enough for you understand the principles behind the technique, which is used all the time by big companies to promote extra sales. Now think how you can set up a test that is both *severe and inexpensive*. You'll create great advertising.

4. Endorsements

The idea of having someone endorse your product is as old as the hills. Probably the best-known of all endorsement campaigns was "*Nine out of ten film stars use Lux*", which ran for years. But since you only have a modest budget, and can't afford a famous personality, how can you use this trusty technique? There are ways. If you can't buy a famous name to drop, don't drop a name at all. Instead, invoke the experience of a group of experts. Let me show you:

* The kind of loaf the baker's wife prefers.

* The hotel that hotel-owners like to stay in.

* The place where travel agents take their holidays.

* The car that chauffeurs like to drive.

* The wine that wine tasters prefer.

* The coffee/tea/fruit juice/brandy/wine tasters prefer.

* The dog-food top breeders use.

* The suit Savile Row tailors admire.

* The pocket-calculator that impresses accountants.

The good thing about this kind of endorsement is if you use it right, you don't have to pay anyone for it. Say you own a men's fashion shop in the High Street, and have some off-the-peg suits to advertise. Get a model to wear one, and have him photographed in the local studio. No need to arrange and pay for a luxury background, you need no background at all. Instead, write over the top of the picture: *What Savile Row tailors admire about my off-the-peg suits.* Then go into the tiny details about how the cut hangs well, lapels are up to the minute, corners of the pocket flaps are gently turned, button holes are finished with five thousand stitches (or whatever), the lapel button hole is ideal for a fresh carnation, the lining helps prevent creasing; you know the kind of thing. You haven't paid any Savile Row tailor, yet you've managed to give your off-the-peg suit the cachet of a bespoke suit. You've pointed out all the benefits of your product, you've even added value to it. That's endorsement advertising, and we know it works.

5. Testimonials

The only difference between the endorsement advertising I've described above, and testimonial advertising, is that for testimonials you need *real* people. But they don't need to be famous, they can be your everyday customers. The advantage of the testimonial is that *it isn't you talking*. If you say your service is good, that's fine, but then who'd expect you to say otherwise? If fifty happy customers say your service is good, that's different. Testimonials are the evidence you're doing something right. Advertisers big and small use them all the time, and the only thing you need to worry about is getting permission from the customers who give you a testimonial that you can use it.

How to use testimonials to best effect? Generally speaking, most advertising simply prints testimonials in ordinary type, and adds a couple of initials at the end. This is fine, but it isn't very credible. If you want the idea to work hard for you, try these techniques:

* Put every testimonial in quote marks.

* Don't set it out in typematter, use handwriting.

* If possible, photograph the original letter you received.

* If the handwriting is poor, and there's the odd spelling mistake, so much the better. It makes the testimonial seem more authentic.

* If you can show a picture of the customer who wrote the letter, terrific. Head and shoulders will do, and it doesn't have to look professional. A snapshot is more believable and costs less. The customer may well give you one.

* Print the customer's full name and address if they'll permit it.

I can't over-emphasise the effectiveness of testimonials. They create powerful advertising. There may even be the odd case where there is nothing to say except quote testimonials. I hope you're not in that position, because then I'd suspect there's not much substance to your product, but a few well-chosen and enthusiastic words really do convince buyers. As I said before they're not the manufacturer talking so they're more credible, and acceptable. The best testimonial advertisement I ever saw showed a picture of Mr Ferrari the racing-ca builder, standing by a small saloon car. The headline read: *Mr Ferrari drives a Fiat.*

6. Demonstration

Demonstration proves usefulness, versatility, how many needs the product satisfies, how often you'll find it wonderful to have around, how it can help in unexpected situations. Most products can be demonstrated if you think about them hard enough, I've even demonstrated the quality of a tinned tomato. Let me explain. H.J. Heinz & Co., that famous (and most conscientious) of companies, invited the agency I worked at to sell a new brand of canned tomatoes. If you look for them on the shelves today you won't find them, but not because they weren't good. The advertising was good, the product was excellent, it just turned out too expensive to launch into a competitive market. This is the story.

Heinz invited me to Portugal, where they were growing marvellous fruit. They'd managed to cultivate a tomato that kept its shape, even after months in the can. If you tip everyday canned tomatoes into a bowl the fruit falls flat. The tomatoes aren't round and firm, they're "deflated". Not so this new brand, they held up. All I had to do was *prove* the superiority. I hit on the idea of "pronging" a Heinz tomato on a fork, holding it in the air (fork-points upwards) and presto – there you had it. The headline simply said: *"New Heinz canned tomatoes. So firm you can prong 'em on a fork".* We added a few words about how they had small hearts, not so many seeds (to get stuck in your teeth) and tasted great, and we had a terrific demonstration advertisement. It ran in colour (colour sells food) and the cans vanished from the shelves. The problem was, to grow such fine tomatoes needs much more *care* than to grow tomatoes for sauce (sauce tommies can be as misshapen as you like). The careful nurturing cost too much money, Heinz couldn't price the new product competitively and it was allowed to die.

Ways to demonstrate your product

* **What** the product does. You can show, in illustrations or photographs, all the things the product will do.

* **Where** the product can do it. You can demonstrate venues where the product is useful. In the car, kitchen, out on a picnic, under the stairs, up a chimney. I leave you to work out the specifics.

* **How** the product works. Illustrate what *makes* it work. How few moving parts there are. How little care and maintenance it needs. How safe it is because of your specially-designed blade (or whatever).

* **When** you'll find the product useful. As soon as you get up in the morning. When you're at a wedding. While you're on holiday. During a snow-storm. Just think of the *times* it helps.

The keynote of a demonstration is SHOW AND TELL how much the product does, how well it does it and how cheaply. You arrive at a demonstration by thinking *how* the customer can benefit. Then, perhaps in a strip cartoon, put the whole thing on paper.

7. Strip Cartoons

Everyone is a sucker for the comic strip. Some newspapers are bought in preference to others because of comic strips. In the USA, the Sunday newspapers run large supplements, full of strips; the *Sunday Mail* stole the idea and brought it to Britain, since they knew it could improve their chances of launching successfully. Comic strips get read – avidly. Use this knowledge to increase the readership of your advertising.

To produce strips you'll need an artist to work from your script. If you can't find one in your district, get in touch with The Association of Illustrators. They have at least 850 members working in UK, and will tell you who's the best comic stripper near your company. Better still they'll give you a list of good artists, experienced at working to a brief. As this book went to press, The Association of Illustrators could be found at 1 Coleville Place, London W1P 1HN, and their telephone number was 071–636 4100. An alternative place to look for local artists is, of course, *Yellow Pages*.

Some advice about producing scripts for a strip cartoon: never repeat information that can be seen from the picture. Always add information in the speech bubbles to the information the picture conveys. Remember it's an accepted convention to switch from a scene of someone using your product in one frame, to a close-up of a hand reaching for the telephone in the next. Keep speech balloons short.

8. Topicality

It frequently happens that your reason to advertise is that you want to link your product or service to a local (or national) event. This is especially true if your company helped to stage the event. You may provide the food, the marquee, put up the scaffolding, flags and bunting, arrange the flowers, provide the band – any of a score of reasons. Obviously you are best judge of whether or not to advertise. Suffice it to say, I believe it's an ideal opportunity to put your name about, since the audience will be able to *see for themselves* how well you did the job.

Let's say there's to be a local event, and your company is involved. It's more than likely the local press will cover the story, and write a column or two, with maybe a picture or two. Well, get your photographer down there taking pictures of what *you do* to make the occasion a success. If the event then *isn't* a success – say it's rained off, or there's a fire, or one of the visitors gets run over by a truck – keep well away. But if all concerned have a great time, then you could buy space in the local paper and put your advertisement in there, with topical pictures, telling your story. And see the paper runs your advertising on the same page as it runs its report. If the idea appeals, let me say it'll take some preparation to set up. You'll have to book the space in the paper, hire the photographer, and get your advertisement "idea" ready *beforehand*. And it's a good thing to have an alternative advertisement standing by in case of unforeseen disasters. Either that, or arrange with the paper that you can postpone using the space.

9. Try this simple test

How often have you been led into a magazine feature by a headline like: "How good a husband/driver/lover/host/guest/holiday companion are you?" Then it goes on to ask a series of questions, and give a series of answers, and you tick the ones that most apply to you. Now you've had it pointed out, you realise this is a journalist's *trick to make you read*; use it in your advertising, we know it works. Here are some headlines that set up the "Test Yourself" technique. You can adapt them to your business.

* **We think this is what makes a great suit.
  See if you agree.**

* **How good a food shopper are you? Test yourself.**

* **How good a judge of furniture are you? Test yourself.**

* **What do you want most from a fireplace? Tick the boxes.
  Then read how ours measures up.**

* **Are these the qualities you look for in a car?**
  Test what you want against what we offer.

* **Ten simple questions to test if you've got a good suit.**

* **Five ways to judge the quality of roast beef.**

You see how the technique is used. Instead of saying: "Here's what we've got for you", you say: "Isn't this what the *definitive* product of our kind should offer?" This format increases the interest and attention value of your publicity. It makes it a good informative read, and invites the reader to pit his wits against yours in deciding what qualities are best in an item. Could he make one any better? Does he own one any better? Hey, reader, don't just sit there, wondering if this product is really what you need, involve yourself in this test.

10. The Guarantee

I'm always surprised by how many companies send out sales material without any reassurance that they're prepared to put their money where their mouth is. The fact is, a guarantee in any sales literature increases the response you get. It bolsters confidence in the product and the company. It reassures readers that if they believe they've been conned and thrown money down the drain, they can have their cash back. All of it without a quibble. Never be afraid to offer a money-back guarantee. Look how well Marks & Spencer do, because customers know they can take anything back and get it changed or get a refund if not entirely satisfied. A guarantee hardly commits you to anything that Common Law doesn't entitle the customer to anyway, and it's an excellent way to convince customers of your integrity.

11. Put yourself in the advertisement

Does this surprise you? Do you buck at the idea that you should sell your product or service *in person*? Will your sales-people think you're a big-head? Does the notion go against the grain? These are perfectly acceptable attitudes, but know this: a number of the biggest and most successful companies in the world – including Schweppes (makers of that famous tonic water), Avis, the car hire company, and a nationally known chicken breeder in the USA (named Frank Perdue) – have created great advertising by featuring the MD or a top salesman in their advertising.

They've done so because it helps to make them more human. It lets the customer come into direct contact with the guy at the top of the tree, the person with the little plaque on his desk that reads: "the buck stops here". That makes the reader feel good. And if it's successful for giant companies, how much more effective is it for a small company, run by a straight-as-a-die boss, determined to offer personal service and see the customer gets what he wants? You're not one of those remote Managing Directors, working out of an ivory tower, who only comes down to staff-level at the Christmas party. You take a shop-floor interest in what goes on, and if anything goes wrong, you'll see it's put right.

Featuring the boss of the company has another advantage, besides personalising the advertising. It lets you write in the first person. That eases up the style, makes it colloquial; you can use phrases you'd use in everyday conversation and they'll sound perfectly natural.

Try this for a sample:

"When I started this company, I swore I'd only work with happy people. Some I hired because of their experience in this business. Some because of their obvious willingness to make the company succeed. All of them were serious, conscientious and not afraid to roll up their sleeves. They've seen the company grow, and this growth has inspired them to keep up their efforts. Success is shared by us all, and the good feeling about work means nothing is ever slipshod or left to chance. The first thing I offer my prospective customer is a workforce with the right attitude."

Already you begin to think you like the sound of this Managing Director. He's the kind of man you'd like to look after your interests. He thinks the way you think, he cares, he's conscientious, you believe you can trust him. Writing your advertising *in the first person* demonstrates how keen you are to get the business. All the same rules apply about seeking out the benefit, making your promise big and bold, all the tips I've included in the book up to this point. This last technique *gives you individuality*, and adds the personal stamp.

C H A P T E R

10

HOW TO DEVISE A GOOD PRESS ADVERTISEMENT.

AND HOW IT WILL BE READ.

"The average advertisement in a newspaper has about 1½ seconds to say. 'Hey, we've got something for you.' After that, the reader moves on."

Stanhope Shelton

CHAPTER TEN

Let's start by defining a "press" advertisement. It's an advertisement which appears in a national or local newspaper or magazine, or in a trade or technical publication. As an advertiser with a smallish budget, you're unlikely to want to buy space in a national newspaper or magazine, since it will cost you an arm and a leg and reach many more customers, over a much wider area, than you need to speak to. However, you may well want to advertise in your local newspaper, or in magazines and journals read by people in your own line of business. Let us recap on when it can be a good idea to buy space in your local (or county) newspaper.

Remember, you must want to advertise to Mr & Mrs Average; the man or woman who buys from a local shop or needs to use a local service. If you make an item, or offer a service that is not used by the general public, then the local newspaper is not for you. If you are a solicitor, optician or accountant, you may argue that your service *is* for the general public. The problem you face is, when is the best *time* to advertise? How can you tell when someone is going to need to consult a solicitor, or need their eyes tested, or need an accountant? You are unlikely to have enough money to advertise in the newspapers on a regular basis. You either run large advertisements, and risk the chance of not being seen at the time your services are needed. Or weekly ones that are so small they might be missed. If you work in any of those professions, I would advise you to consider other media to reach your audience. A solicitor, for example, has a very good, and detailed, case to present. Yet he is unlikely to have a fortune to spend on selling his service. Consider direct mail, that is a letter, accompanied by a more detailed brochure, which you can address *personally* to your audience, and so be certain they'll get the message.

First do your homework

How do you decide which local newspaper? Simple, you get in touch with the space representative and invite him to come and talk to you. You find out where in the district the paper goes, how many readers it reaches and what kind of people they are (men, women, rich, poor, how old, and so on). Then ask for the rate-card, which will give you the costs for the various sizes of space available. Before he leaves, ask the rep to send you a copy of the paper, if he hasn't brought one with him.

When you have the paper in front of you, look through it to see where you would like to appear. You can decide which page, according to the kind of editorial that appears on the page. If you run a Video-Store, for example, a good idea is to buy space on the entertainments page. A fashion-shop, then the woman's page is for you. If you are a solicitor, then choose a page where the ediotrial is of a serious nature, say the leader or correspondence page. This "serious" editorial will reflect the seriousness of your message.

The space you buy

Obviously the larger space you buy, the more it costs. But in a local paper you should plump for as big a space as you can afford, since many advertisers can afford to buy, and a large size will reflect the importance of your message and the size of your business. It's better to be "king-for-a-day" than disappear into the morass of smaller advertisers and risk not being seen at all. Once you're happy that you've found the right page for your advertisement, decide on the exact size of space you want then trace the space onto your layout pad. If you choose to run your ad on a right-hand page, any coupon should go in the bottom right-hand corner. Ads on a left-hand page demand coupons in the left-hand corner. This way they can be cut out without decimating either the rest of your advertisement, or the newspaper.

Work in the space you've got

When you've got your space drawn out on your layout pad, you can do one of two things. You can write your advertisement directly into that space. Or you can draw out a much larger space – in *direct proportion* to the one you've bought – and work in that. Working within your space helps in a number of ways. You know how many words you can get in, and how big they'll appear. You can "see" how big your pictures are likely to be. This matters because you can't reproduce very small photographs in local newspapers, they simply appear as a splodge, because the ink "spreads" and the photo becomes fudged. A way round this is to use fine line illustrations; this means you'll have to commission an artist to draw your picture for you. *Working within the space* also shows how much room you'll need for the application form, how big you can afford to have the company name, whether you can put a small map in the ad (to show how to get to the store) or whether to settle for the address and telephone number only.

CHAPTER TEN

Working to the area you've got concentrates the mind, and makes you economise on words and include only the essentials of what you have to say. It's a natural thought, when you work like this, to believe you haven't got enough room to get everything in you want to, but don't despair. Typematter is very easy to read in a quite small size – consult the editorial columns of your paper for confirmation of this. Just by counting the words in one column of type, you can get the measure of how much space you need. And don't fall into the trap of wanting to make everything big. The main emphasis should be on your headline, that is, the offer you make to entice readers into the advertisement. This may seem to be a fiddly way of working, but it does help. Having your local paper beside you will show you how other people advertise, how the editor lays out his stories, how coupons and application forms are written and designed, the kind (and size) of pictures used, where the address and telephone numbers go, and so on.

Run-of-paper or special position?

There are two ways of buying space. One is called run-of-paper, that is you buy a set size, but you appear where the newspaper wants to put you. The second way is to negotiate a special position, and this means you can specify where in the newspaper your advertisement is to be placed. Negotiating a special position costs you a little more, depending on the demand for that particular space. Many newspapers run a single advertisement at the bottom right-hand corner of the *front page*, and it is generally the only advertisement on the front page, if you exclude the "ear-spaces" which are the tiny advertisements on either side of the paper's mast-head (or title). This *front-page solus* is generally in high demand, since it is normally used, on a regular basis, by one or two dominant advertisers. But if you think it might be good for you, you can always ask when the space is next available. If the *front-page solus* isn't booked and you decide to use it, it will cost you a little over the odds.

Stick to the system

When you get down to making your advertisement, stick to the system described in the previous chapters. You must know *what* your offer is, *who* you're talking to, and both these things must be clear in your headline. You then proceed to make the rest of your case the way a good advocate does, with reasoned argument and simple words. Working in the exact type-area imposes a discipline on you. You can't be verbose, you have to cut your copy to the size of space available. Go back over the rules on how to arrive at your headline (Chapter 5) and try out a number of ways of expressing the promise. Check too Chapter 6, on writing body copy. Remember how useful small cross-headings can be in breaking up the text. Follow the discipline and you'll get it right.

How advertisements are read

Not suprisingly, advertising agencies are interested in how their work is read, and have carried out research to discover how the reader behaves. They found that people have a habitual way of approaching advertisements. I'll go through it, step by step, because when you know the route the eye takes, you're better armed to do your job.

The first place a reader's eye looks when he comes to an ad is at the picture. The photograph of the product – or whatever – is seen right at the start. Then the eye goes to the headline. Finally it drops to the bottom right-hand corner of the ad to see who's paying the bill.

And that's how far most readers get
with most advertisements.

Sobering thought, eh? Well, here's one to make you more sober. Out of five or six hundred advertisements which bombard us every day, from newspapers, magazines, buses, poster-sites, TV, radio, and shop windows, the average person remembers between seven and ten. That's what the researchers tell us, and if they tell us true, then a lot of companies are spending a lot of advertising money and not getting much in return. Working to a format helps you become one of those ten ads remembered.

Where the eye goes next

Sometimes, in ads, there is a caption in small italic type, under the picture, the way newspapers caption their photographs. The caption describes something about the picture. That's where the eye goes next. Then if your advertisement contains cross-headings in a bolder type-face, or a smaller illustration, or thumbnail sketch, that's where the eye goes next. Finally, if you've kept the reader's interest thus far, he'll reach the first line of the body copy. And from then on, if you've written in an interesting manner, he'll follow your argument through to the last full stop. That, according to the best research, is how most people come to most advertisements. One other fact that'll emphasise the hardness of your task is, as a general rule you have just *1½ seconds* to declare your message. Copywriters in most agencies know this is what they're up against, and for that reason alone stick to known techniques.

So what?

Now we have this information, let's go back and see what it can teach us about filling in the square on our layout pad. The reader's eye goes to the picture first, so the more of the story you get into the picture the better. Generally speaking the thing to make clear immediately is what you're selling, and usually it's a product, so the picture should be a photograph of the product. But what if it isn't a product? Unless I know your business I can't tell you exactly, so let me list the twelve subjects most likely to make people read. If you buy any popular newspaper, you'll find from eight to ten of these subjects covered virtually every day; readers never tire of them. How does the editor keep his audience glued to the page? By talking about the following:

1. Animals	4. Disasters	7. Money	10. Sport
2. Babies	5. Entertainment	8. Royalty	11. War
3. Cars	6. Fashion	9. Sex	12. Weddings

I hold the view that if you take any popular paper for one year you will have read everything it's ever going to print. From year two, only the people, places and number of the dead and wounded change. Certainly I believe if all the world's news dried up tonight, most of our press wouldn't notice.

At this stage you might ask which of these subjects is most pertinent to your business, and how do you know the one to choose? Well, there's one you *can't* choose, and that's Royalty. We are forbidden to feature any of the Royal family in publicity. As for the other subjects, your choice depends on the audience you're talking to. The advertising rule of thumb is, if you're talking to women, you should show women in your picture, if to men, then feature men, if to pensioners, pensioners, and so on. But you can also use the subjects that *interest* women: animals, babies, weddings, christenings, fashion. And the subjects that *interest* men: sport, money, cars, war, natural disasters such as typhoons, earthquakes, volcanoes. And the subjects that interest almost everybody: entertainment, film and TV stars, famous personalities of all kinds, and, of course, sex.

A plea for discrimination

It is the practice in some circles to use sex to sell almost anything, and who hasn't seen advertisements featuring topless models hugging the product to their bosoms, or displaying their charms across cars, desk tops, and so forth? Sometimes this can be done effectively, as in the case of the famous Unipart calendars, and indeed I doubt if there's an office or works canteen in Britain which doesn't hang somewhere a calendar showing half-clad pretty girls. Nothing wrong with that; indeed they cheer up a warehouse or factory floor no end. But I would ask you to think before using the same technique in newspaper and magazine advertising. At best, a semi-nude girl is "borrowed-interest" and at worst it's a crude piece of sexism, which won't reflect well on your company and will leave you and your sales force open to mockery. Just a little thought can bring you a more apposite illustration and prevent you from falling into work that insults the reader's intelligence and harms your business image.

Lazy pictures

Using sex to sell is lazy, but there is more than one form of lazy picture; I mean the kind of illustration that you see so often. The kind that becomes a visual cliché, and as such, fails to attract attention. One of them is what I describe as the "Kitchener-needs-you" picture, a stern-looking face and raised right hand, with finger pointing straight out of the ad into your face. How many times have you seen that? Another one is the montage (turn again to page 94), and some advertisers are drawn to it because they believe they must illustrate everything. Thus you get a kind of "film-poster" effect, with the factory, the product, a train, plane or truck, a computer, a telephone and heaven-knows-what else all melded together. It's a natural "first thought", but when it pops into your mind I urge you to discard it. You'll note that editors never use montages. Other lazy pictures include thumbs-up signs, cartoon Supermen, pieces of paper fastened with paper-clips and bees making a bee-line for something. Once you've thought of them, think again.

Phase two of the eye-journey

After the picture, the reader's eye goes to the headline, and this is the acid test to see whether you can hold attention or not. We spent Chapter 5 discussing ways to arrive at the best headline, so I won't go through any of that again. Suffice to remind you with a checklist:

CHAPTER TEN

1. Do you know what you want to say?

2. Does your headline have a big promise?

3. Is it written in a pithy way?

4. Is it easy to understand?

5. Have you used short, Anglo-Saxon words?

6. Do the words relate to the picture?

7. Have you included the name of the product?

8. Is your promise in any way unique?

9. If your wife read it, would she believe it?

10. Have you created a "telegram"?

Remember, your product or service contains a promise; If it wasn't so you'd already be out of business. You're inviting someone to trade; you've got something you believe they want, you're presenting it in an interesting, memorable way. You're identifying (and answering) their needs. They stand to gain if they buy, all you do is tell them how and why.

Getting into the small print

After the headline, the reader looks to see which company is running the ad, and the eye goes to the bottom right-hand corner of the space. Put the name of the company there. A good way to leave the name uncluttered is to put the other important details, address, telephone and telex numbers at the end of the body text. And leave a little "air" between the "logo" (your trade mark) and the last lines of the copy, so it stands out clean and clear.

How to make the eye-journey easier

There are lots of little "tricks" that keep the customer reading. They include the use of brief sub-headings, to break up your copy into paragraphs. Or you can pop in a small line drawing, to demonstrate a selling point, or emphasise some fact better described in pictures than words. Graphs, charts and diagrams help too, so does a drop-capital-letter at the beginning of the copy, and indenting the subsequent paragraphs. Try and set out your text matter in reasonable-width columns. Remember most of us are used to reading text no more than two inches wide. Quotation marks, italic type, bold type and underlining are other ways to add interest, but be careful not to be too liberal with them, or you'll end up with a mass of words that looks "spotty" and takes away from the "quality" feel of your work. Finally, don't be misled into thinking that you need a huge company name to sign off. Provided it's where it should be, and has space around it, the customer will know who's talking to him.

A CHECKLIST

1. Get copies of the newspaper or magazine in which your advertisement is to appear.

2. Look out an advertisement the same size as yours.

3. Draw up that space on your layout pad.

4. Think of your headline first.

5. Think of the picture you're going to use.
   Remember, one picture is better than several.

6. Men look at men, women at women, pensioners at pensioners. It's a way to show who you're talking to.

7. Remember the eye-journey. (a) picture (b) headline (c) name of company, and so on.

A HORROR STORY

In March 1984, the 10-year-running BBC Radio 4 programme "Checkpoint" broadcast the following story. I shall not name the individual concerned, although "Checkpoint" had no such qualms.

Mr X, worked as an increasingly successful salesman on a freesheet newspaper. Intoxicated by this success, he began to place advertisements in the paper, without his customers' permission, then invoiced them for space they hadn't booked. The fraud was discovered and he was fired.

He started his own paper and the skulduggery continued. Worse, he invoiced advertisers for double the amount of advertising, after it had appeared (without their permission). He then began to cut the print-run of the paper. Fewer than half the number he claimed were printed, were being distributed. He refused to pay journalists and the content of the papers was reduced to advertising exclusively. He defrauded printers and when they asked for their money, moved to fresh ones.

He began to produce freesheet magazines and the same frauds applied. He sold phoney shares to his employees. Finally, when all this caught up with him, the papers and magazines (and the money they made) disappeared, along with Mr X and his "shareholders'" savings.

Mr X is still at large, and producing freesheets and magazines somewhere in the UK. You have been warned.

CHAPTER 11

EIGHT COMMON WAYS TO ADVERTISE ON A LOW BUDGET.

"Forget what you want to write, remember what the reader wants to read."

John Frazer-Robinson

"Any fool can write a sales-letter - and too many do."
Brian Holland Ad-Agency Owner

Thus far we've considered the making of a sales brochure, writing a press advertisement and have looked at some tested advertising techniques. Which leaves a fair number of other kinds of advertising still to be discussed, and in this chapter I want to cover those to use if you don't have much money to spend. The thought I want to introduce at the start is, *if you have something to say, say it.* It may surprise you to learn that a great deal of money is spent on advertising where the writer has nothing to say. For example, what can you tell a housewife about baked beans that she doesn't already know? What can you tell a beer-drinker, who downs half-a-dozen pints in one session, about his favourite brew that he doesn't already know? What is there to say about boiled sweets, except that they taste nice and come in a variety of flavours? What is there to say about shampoo, except it leaves your hair squeaky-clean and sweet-smelling? Yet the makers of these products spend millions of pounds advertising them, and the people who make the TV commercials have to *find* something to say.

That's not your problem

Happily, since you make a product (or offer a service) unlike those mentioned above, you do *not* find yourself in the position of having nothing to say. Quite the contrary, you may find you have too much to say to cram it all into one small advertisement, and it's a question of reducing your message to the relevant sales points. So I do not propose to talk about the techniques of writing sales material where you have nothing to say. In a position like that the keynote is "showmanship"; people who write for Heineken or Hamlet Cigars are almost in the entertainment business. Of course advertising can entertain, and most TV viewers look forward to the commercials that make them laugh. Although this kind of advertising is the sort most frequently talked about over the dinner-table, it's not where you should be. You're advertising because you have something to say, so the rule you must follow is very simple: *Say it.*

RADIO COMMERCIALS.

At first glance the radio commercial is very attractive to the local business. Costs are low, time is usually available and the price to produce your advertisement is low. The news the station plays is localised, and a general cheery atmosphere prevails. Before you decide to broadcast, however, I want you to ask:

* Who are you talking to?

* What kind of atmosphere do you want to create?

* How "serious" is your message?

Let us remind ourselves of the general nature of the local radio audience – it tends to be female, in the younger age groups and down-market. This makes it ideal for shops and stores, household goods, soaps, detergents, toothpastes, some local fashions, food, and so on. It could be argued that you can reach male listeners as they drive to and from work. Yes, if they haven't got the BBC switched on. Check with your local station how many men they're reaching and what class and age groups. In general, if you listen to local radio, you'll know that Tesco, with the best price-deals, is perfectly at home there. I would need to be thoroughly convinced, however, before I advertised a solicitor or an optician using radio commercials.

What kind of commercial?

I once met an American who "knew" without question what kind of commercials worked on radio. They were "slices-of-life" or threesome-conversations, either a man and two women or a woman and two men, chatting in a friendly, natural manner. The commercial opened with a hook – that is, one of the characters would say something that would stop the listener dead – like: "The pig just died!" Then the dialogue expands on the "problem", in this case pig-plague or whatever. The second character soon takes up the conversation: "But haven't you heard of 'Pig-saver?'" "Pig-saver – sounds interestin', but what is it and how much?" This part of the commercial presents the "solution" to the previously presented "problem". Enter the third character, with the "proof". "Golly-gosh yes, farmer Giles has been usin' Pig-saver and now his pigs have wings." Although I'm sending the style up, don't laugh too loud: done with skill and professionalism it works, and this American has millions to prove it. But he was selling diet-aids, and anti-dandruff shampoos, where there was a "problem" and the product was the "solution" and because-I-say-so was the "proof".
What happens with different kinds of products and services? Well, you can try the slice-of-life route, but I'd also like to suggest the following.

* If you've got something to say, like money-off or new shop

opens today, SAY IT.

* If it's an ordinary product – sausages, new suits, double-glazing – MAKE 'EM LAUGH. And while you do so, make them remember the name.

* Remember, you're dealing with a "sound" medium. Use as much SOUND as you can.

The secret is that you've got between 10 and 60 seconds to make an impression and here's the kind of radio dialogue that gets remembered. First voice (harshly)! "Your money or your life?" Pause, held until the waiting is so unbearable you begin to think the radio is on the blink. Then the robber screams again: "Your money or your life?" And the victim screams back: "I'm thinking about it!" That's the essence of a memorable radio commercial.

Use the local radio if you have a NEWS announcement to make. Your prices are down, you've got a special offer just arrived, your new branch is being opened this morning. Or use it as REMINDER advertising, if you've been established for ever, the community knows about you, and you can play your song "At McDonald's we've got time for you", or whatever. But if you want your listeners to remember you can, in my view, forget about the radio commercial. Nor have I ever written down an address or phone number after hearing a radio-spot.

Finally it's worth remembering that when you use radio, your local station will almost certainly make the commercial for you, and provide you with the announcer to read your message and as many sound effects as your script is likely to need – they have a whole library full, from the chuff-chuff-whistle of the Coronation Scot as it climbs the gradient to the Border, to smashing glass and falling masonry as the nuclear war begins.

Trade and technical advertising

The trade and technical press carries mostly serious, informative advertising, the exceptions being where a particular company is so well known, and the goods it offers so well understood, that the function of the advertisement is to remind readers that the company and its products are alive, well and looking for business. What steps should you take when advertising in the trade and technical journals?

DO YOUR OWN ADVERTISING

The first thing is to buy a copy of each journal you plan to use, and read it. Start at the back, at the recruitment pages. The ads here will tell you about the readers. The kind of companies they work in, what their responsibilities are, what qualifications they have, and even the kind of money they earn. Then turn to the leader in the magazine. Here you'll find the issues of the day and you may be able to tie a particular topic into your advertisement. Then you can check the news and feature pages; this will give you a look into current events in the business lives of the readers. Finally, check the existing advertisements; if they're any good they should give you a guide to how technical you can be when you write, the tone of voice to use, who your main competitors are and the kind of offers they are making.

Where's your advertisement going?

By which I mean, in what *part* of the magazine – what kind of space have you bought, in what position? Good positions include next to the contents column, next to the leader, the inside front (or back) cover and the outside back cover, or the first right-hand page of advertising. These are known as special positions and you'll generally have to pay more for them than for a "run-of-paper" space. However, you're buying higher "traffic". For example, it's fairly certain readers will scan the contents list of the magazine, so your advertisement opposite – or alongside – has a greater chance of being seen and read. Personally, if I have to advertise on either the inside or outside of the magazine cover, I try to keep my message as simple and speedy as possible. Not many readers study the back page, so you have to reach them quickly and tell your story fast.

Now follow the discipline set out in chapter ten. Draw out the space you have to work in, decide your headline, decide your picture – which will normally be a picture of the product – and write out your message, remembering the most important point to communicate is what you are offering. When your complete case has been set out, decide what you want the reader to do. Spell that out carefully, putting a coupon at the bottom if you have free literature to offer, together with your telephone number and the name of someone to speak to. One final exhortation: please stick to facts. Words like exciting, amazing, incredible, superb, outstanding, are wearisome to read and carry no conviction. The reader will respect you more if you give pure information.

CHAPTER ELEVEN

Sales-letters

You may be asking whether it is best to send your customer a leaflet telling about your product, or a sales-letter. When it's a case of one or the other, a sales-letter is best; people like getting letters, and the more they get, the more they respond. Here are the basic answers to the most usually asked questions.

What kind of envelope should you use?

An envelope with a window wins greater response than an envelope without one. Coloured envelopes increase reader-interest.

Where should the address go?

Either at the top of the letter you're sending, or on an enclosed reply-paid card. If you're sending both, then plump for the reply-paid card. This means the reader doesn't have to write out his address before he returns the card, and all you have to do is ask him to check it to make sure it's correct.

Should you print on the envelope?

Yes, you should. You're paying for the space, so use it. Also a message printed on the envelope helps tell the post-room (or secretary) who the letter is for, why it should be delivered, and what's the promise for the reader. A good promise on the outside of the envelope will stimulate interest and pull in more replies.

Are sales-letters written to a format?

Yes, they are, and it's a format you've probably heard. A sales-letter develops in five stages. 1. Attract attention. 2. Create interest. 3. Stimulate desire – make the reader *want*. 4. Create conviction. 5. Incite action – that is, tell the reader what you want him to do. In any sales letter you write, always *lead with your offer*.

What about layout?

Sales-letters should be laid out in short paragraphs. It's a good idea to indent each paragraph. And when you get to an important point, underline that sentence using a second colour.

How long should it be?

There's a worry among newcomers to sales-letters that they'll make them too long. Don't worry about it. I've heard of successful letters that went on for eight pages. Four pages is quite common, three could be enough, two or fewer and you probably haven't stated your benefits sufficiently, rung the changes on them enough, emphasised your promises in four or five different ways.

Keep the reader moving

In Chapter 6, I gave you a list of link-phrases: *that's only part of it... just as important...not to mention...moreover...we couldn't end without.* Use these phrases to urge the reader on. Remember when you get to the bottom of the first page, make your last sentence run over onto page two. Or, if it doesn't work out like that, say "Please turn over".

Come to the convincing part

When you've made your case as clearly as you can, think what questions your reader will ask. What doubts might have arisen in his mind? What other information does he need? Then answer the questions, assuage the doubts, provide the final *facts* that convince him your deal is sound.

Finally, the action part

It can happen, even when you've succeeded thus far, that the reader will put off taking any action until later that day. Then, life being what it is, something else captures his attention and your letter is forgotten. Ways to get an immediate response include putting an "Offer must end ... date" in your final paragraph." Or, "Get your secretary to post the reply card now, while it's still fresh in your mind."

Recruitment advertising

The advantage a recruitment advertisement has over most other kinds is that readers are *looking for it.* The recruitment pages are some of the most thoroughly read in the magazine, and the cost of the space reflects that. Remember, too, you'll be surrounded by many other recruitment ads, so the first thing you must do is flag your audience. Lead with the job you have to offer. A headline that says: GRADUATE TO TEACH MATHEMATICS AND COMPUTER STUDIES is much better than OUTSTANDING OPPORTUNITY TO TEACH 14/16 YEAR OLDS AT PUBLIC SCHOOL.

Once you've flagged the person you want, talk about *them.* The qualifications they'll need, the degree of experience, the kind of attitude you expect, the salary and the fringe benefits (car, medical insurance, pension scheme, four weeks' paid holiday). It's better to make the job seem difficult rather than easy, the work demanding and the effort required out-of-the-ordinary, than to minimise obstacles. This flatters the gifted applicant and weeds out the insecure.

Then talk about yourself. The size of the company, its standing in the market, the environment, work colleagues, reputation, quality of goods to be sold. Give the salary, I can never understand why so many companies don't; they must know what they expect to pay. Nobody earning more will apply, those earning less know what's expected of them to deserve the kind of jump in pay you offer. Avoid box numbers, it makes applicants suspicious. If you use a headhunter, reassure applicants that they won't be reported to the boss if the company they apply to is their own. Avoid meaningless waffle: "Salary will be commensurate with applicant's experience". Of course it will. Put a date by which applications must be received. Don't write anything that doesn't increase the *information* you impart either about the applicant, or what's in the job for them. Over-writing puts off intelligent job-hunters and reflects badly on your company.

Classified advertising

Classified pages are divided into sections, so first check which section is most appropriate for your ad. The CARS column, the WANTED column, the FOR SALE column, EVERYTHING UNDER £20, or whatever.

There are four kinds of classified advertisement. The lineage advertisement, which looks as style one (see page 158) and in which, usually you must buy a minimum of two lines, which average out about five words a line. A lineage advertisement, style two which allows you a headline and an additional line of white space above and below to help attract attention. A semi-display classified (style three), differentiated by a black line above and below, and a classified display advertisement (style four). Box numbers are usually charged as an extra and you can buy at discount rates if you book a fixed number of consecutive insertions. For advice on how to get the most from a classified ad ring the advertise*ment* (note, *not* the advertis*ing*) department. Or follow the tips given here.

Find out the minimum number of lines you must buy. Head up your advertisement with the name of the product you want to sell. If it's a car, say '85 **VOLVO**, '82 **ROVER** or whatever. Do not start

WHAT YOU NEED TO KNOW

STYLES AND RATES

STYLE 1

THIS IS A LINEAGE advertisement. It is charged per line, with a minimum size of two lines. There are approximately four words per line.

STYLE 2

THIS STYLE IS as above with the addition of one line of white space above and below to draw further attention to the classified advertisement. The minimum size for this style is four lines.

STYLE 3

KNOWN AS

SEMI DISPLAY

This style is differentiated by a black line above and below the advertisement. One or two columns may be used with a minimum size in both cases of three centimetres per column. This type of advertisement is charged per single column centimetre.

STYLE 4

THIS IS A CLASSIFIED DISPLAY ADVERTISEMENT

It is contained within its own distinctive border and has the same minimum sizes quoted for semi-display. Photographs, name blocks and company logos may be used in Classified Display, which is charged per single column centimetre.

SUPERB CONDITION or ONE OWNER since the reader first seeks the product he's looking for, and only when he's found that, wants to know details. If the column is headed WANTED, don't start your ad with WANTED. Likewise if the column is headed FOR SALE. If the column is headed MUSIC, start with the name of the instrument you offer, if it's headed HOLIDAYS, start with the place. When you write stick to facts; you haven't got the space to persuade, only inform. Don't suggest "or near offer" generally abbreviated to o.n.o. Once you get a buyer, that's the time to negotiate, and he might be prepared to pay what you're asking. Always negotiate and if he thinks the price you're asking for your fish tank (for example) is too high, throw in some pond weed, tank gravel or filter as an extra incentive. If the buyer thinks he's getting those items as "free extras", then he'll be happier to pay your asking price. Ask the publication you're using for help, there's almost always a bright young girl or man working in the classified department who knows how to compose effective classified ads; since their brainpower comes free, use it.

Bus and tube advertising

First, bus advertising, which can appear outside or inside the bus. Outside you've only space for a few words, and they must include the name of your product or company. Don't clutter them up with your address, telephone number and the name of the MD's wife. Write the message a dozen or so ways and try them out on colleagues to see which is best. On the inside you have a longer time to tell your story, since the audience is riding with you, with nowhere to look except at the head of the passenger in front. The rules for the inside of buses also apply if you're composing cards for tube trains. Glasgow Underground spent £43 millions on a refurbishing programme, to make the stations and trains brighter and quieter. At present Glasgow has 33 carriages in service and each displays ten advertisement cards. The system is designed to carry, ultimately, over 25 million passengers a year. If you want to advertise on it, get in touch with Primesight Ltd. Their London office is at 10 Lower Grosvenor Place, London, SW1W 0EN, telephone 071-834 9801, and they also have offices in Manchester and Glasgow. The London Underground is a much bigger system with many more advertising options. To advertise on it consult London Transport Advertising, 26 Jamestown Road, Camden, London NW1 7BY, telephone 071-482 3000.

Handbills

Too many companies start off with a cheap paper, print only on one side, restrict the information they give to a few brief lines, use no illustrations, leave no name for the prospect to get in touch with, and I have known occasions where the job was done so badly the advertiser even forgot to include his telephone number, which he added later with a rubber stamp. Thus the message communicates so badly, and brings such a poor response, that their worst suspicions are confirmed and they never venture into advertising again.

The handbill is a medium frequently used by a new company, just setting up in business and hoping to make an impression in the local community. The question is, what kind of an impression do you want to make? You should want people to believe you are a *top quality company*, offering outstanding service, or with an outstanding product to sell. The keynote is quality, and the way to convey that message is not to spoil the ship for ha'porth of tar. I know you haven't got millions, but I do recommend you buy a good-quality card on which to send your message. Quality paper denotes a quality company. Next, never starve your customer of information. You're going to have to

C. PLUMBRIDGE
(Established 1969)

ANTIQUE AND HOUSEHOLD REMOVALS

—◆※◆—

TRADE DELIVERIES AND COLLECTIONS

—◆※◆—

COMPLETE HOUSE CLEARANCES

—◆※◆—

SECONDHAND FURNITURE BOUGHT

—◆※◆—

DISTANCE NO OBJECT

—◆※◆—

COMPETITIVE PRICES

—◆※◆—

FREE ESTIMATES

—◆※◆—

01 - 398 6442   Phone Day or Night   **01 - 398 6958**

How not to do it
This handbill, on cheap paper with two rubber-stamped phone numbers (which do you use?) is an example of how to throw away advertising money. There is no promise, a minimum of information, and no directions to the customer as to what he should do. The reverse side was totally blank.

give the job to a printer, and it hardly makes much difference to him whether he prints fifty words or two hundred and fifty. Provided your opening gambit is interesting enough, your prospect will spend as long as he likes taking in the rest of the story. After all, he's at leisure, in his own home, so have the courage to present your case in some detail, and write it at a good level of intelligence.

I shudder to think how often I've got handbills through my letter box which look as if and the writer hardly *expects* a response. Little line illustrations, supporting sales points are cheap to commission and pay off by increasing interest and readability. If your printer sets up

How to get the maximum impact and information into the minimum space.
This handbill sells its heart out.

your handbill himself, at least persuade him to use a professional typographer to choose the type for you, and set it out tastefully.

Of course all the rules about pinpointing the customer, picking out the promise, and convincing readers they've found a good deal still apply. Always print on both sides of your card; only *make it clear which is side one* and which side two. To do that you print your main headline, in bigger type on side one, and number side two. Handbills needn't be shots in the dark which may or may not hit home. If you take them seriously they'll produce serious results.

Although you may be using low-budget media, the thinking should be of a high calibre. One of the top agency men in the USA said that

the right approach to advertising can make $500 work as hard a
$5,000; you can't vary the cost of producing your advertising by much
but you can vary the effectiveness, and that's done by treating the jo
seriously and with enthusiasm.

12

STEALING FROM THE EDITORS.

FIVE PROVEN WAYS TO MAKE YOUR ADVERTISING MORE INTERESTING.

"I have six honest serving men,
They taught me all I knew,
Their names are what and why and when,
And how and where and who."

Rudyard Kipling

The message to take away from the next few pages is this: it takes no more time to create advertising which is good and interesting, than it takes to create advertising which is bad and boring. And it takes no more money to run the first kind than the second. If you run advertising people want to read, you get results, so everything you can do to increase the readership of your material is worth hard cash. The big agencies make a point of this when they vie for business, and one of them puts it as follows.

"It's an old maxim that the best kind of advertising is word of mouth. Unfortunately you can't buy space in this medium. At least not with money. How you can buy it is with advertising that gets noticed. The more it gets noticed, the more it gets talked about, and the more it gets talked about the more it gets noticed. That kind of advertising is the most cost-effective you can buy. The amazing thing is, that it doesn't actually cost any more than advertising that doesn't get noticed and talked about".*

How do you create interest?

What can you do to make your advertising the kind people want to read; the kind they notice and talk about? One answer is, steal. When the editor sends his reporters out on a job, they don't come back unless they've found answers to six things.

1. What is the event?

2. Where did it happen?

3. How did it happen?

4. When did it happen?

5. Why did it happen?

6. Who made it happen – and to whom?

Those are the things that make you read. You can put this to the test, now, by finding a newspaper or colour-supplement and checking the following. How many of the features begin with the word HOW? As in "*How Blank won the Grand Prix*", or "*How Maximus Incorporated took over Minimus Incorporated*", or "*How Silly Billy cheated the Breathalyser.*" And how many features and headlines begin with WHY? As for the photographs, ninety-nine times out of a hundred

* The credo of ad-agency Gold Greenlees Trott.

they're of people, in other words WHO. Editors follow these techniques and teach them to cub reporters because they *work*.

What this means to advertisers

I would commend to you that next time you read a paper, do so with those six words in mind. And as you scan the headlines of features, and of the advertisements, make a mental note of the number that start with one of these six words. Soon you'll get the hang of the techniques and how they can lead to very interesting headlines for your own publicity. At the beginning of this book there's a copy of an advertisement for Dale Carnegie's *How to win friends and influence people*. And you suddenly notice that even the book title has got the word HOW in it, and if you turn back to the advertisement you'll be amazed at the number of times these six little words appear. We're all so used to these writing techniques, we don't notice them. But when pointed out they offer a great way to add interest and intrigue to your writing.

Ways to use the HOW technique

The usual practice is to begin your headline with the words HOW TO. Just adding these two little words makes all the difference. For example, if I exhort you to "*Win a holiday in the Bahamas*" then you'll probably think sure, very nice, but I never win contests so I won't bother to enter. But if I change this headline to "*How to win a holiday in the Bahamas*", then I'm promising to tell you something, and I'm also offering help, and with help comes hope that you could win. Thus the interest value is increased, there's a reward for reading and so you're coaxed in. The other fact about using HOW TO at the beginning of your headline is that it gives you the chance to explain. You're promising to tell all the different aspects of your story.

Practical example No. 1

Let's say you run a small private catering service. You plan menus, prepare and cook food, provide wines, crockery, cutlery, condiments and so on, set the table with linen, flowers and appropriate glassware, then deliver the meal and let the host and hostess take things from there, while you and your staff disappear into the background, coming out only when the guests have retired and it's time to clear the debris. You can sum your offer up in a single line, if you use the HOW TO technique.

How to host the perfect dinner-party.
How to become a cordon-bleu cook for a day.
How to dine à-la-Maxims, without going there.
How to have the perfect celebratory meal.

Practical example No. 2

Let's say you design, make and install open-hearth fireplaces, the kind that went out of fashion as people became able to afford full central heating, and came back into fashion again when they began to miss the focal point to the room. Your fireplaces come in a range of styles and run on gas. Your company does the complete job and leaves the householder with virtually a new room. You could have a brochure, the front cover of which reads, "The Cosy Range of Fireplaces". But how much more interesting and inviting your sales pitch becomes if you headline your brochure with:

How to find the ideal fireplace for your home.
How to turn the room in your head into a room in your house
How to bring a new heart to your living room.
How to rekindle your hearth.

Practical example No. 3

Not so long ago, my local antique dealer dropped a leaflet through our door, asking if he could come and take a look round my home. Perhaps I had some antiques which, unknown to me, were worth a lot of money. The piece was dull, and it seemed all he wanted was a snoop. Yet genuine treasures have been discovered in attics and storerooms, which when brought to light and sold, earned a pretty sum of money. The point here is, the antique dealer needed to do a little homework, and discover examples of where antiques were recovered, and householders became richer. It shouldn't be hard to find such examples, especially if you work in the trade. Then, showing one or two items (no Hogarths or Constables, please), together with their true values, my antique dealer could have prepared the same leaflet, and printed it for the same cost, with headlines like:

How to find hidden treasure in your home.
How to enjoy an unexpected windfall this year.
How to make the most of what seems the least.

Making the most of the technique

Now you understand the way it's used adapt this technique to your product or service. I'm not saying you can apply HOW TO automatically but clearly the HOW TO beginning to a headline offers possibilities. Let's say you offer a garden-care service. You can promote it more imaginatively with:

How to have colour in your garden 52 weeks a year.

Say you run a delivery service, and you have motor-cycles and pick-up vans which collect and deliver articles of all kinds. Since the Post Office also handles such material, your plus must be that you work fast. A little imagination and you can convince your customers you really care, and have the right attitude and sense of urgency. Indeed, you treat every parcel like it was wanted yesterday. So you say:

How to get an urgent parcel delivered yesterday.

Say you run a local garage, and one source of income is your car repair service. You work conscientiously, have a number of regular customers and your staff is competent and loyal. You could prepare a leaflet urging drivers to come to Joe's Garage. Or you could say something like:

How to make your car look younger, last longer and sell easier.

Say you're going into business as a greengrocer, and you want to show you have an edge on the competition. It's not likely that you'll ever do regular advertising but you could run an advertisement announcing your opening and say:

How to tell how fresh things are.

One final example to demonstrate the breadth of the technique. Let's say you offer a double-glazing service, or a home insulation service, or both. You know all about stopping draughts and heat loss, and insulating those places where heat escapes, but the householder never thinks about. The truth of this matter is that the house is stealing money because it's so leaky. And you can save the householder from this loss with your complete service. What about a leaflet that begins:

How to make sure you're not living with a thief.

Ways to use the WHY technique

Just as HOW can improve your copywriting skill, so can WHY. It was never demonstrated more clearly for me than when a pharmaceutical company launched the toothpaste *Signal*, the one (if you remember) that had the mouthwash in the stripes. At the launch of this advertising, the toothpaste itself was interesting because never before had a maker devised a way of laying red stripes down a white paste (it was done, as we all soon found out, by putting a colorant into the neck of the tube). So all they had to do in the early advertising was to say: "*Signal has a mouthwash in the stripes*", and to show pictures of this amazing two-coloured paste. But gradually the idea became commonplace, and the advertising had to find a new way of getting attention and persuading us the stripe was doing its job. Few of us believed a film of colorant actually had much effect. However, nothing daunted, the ad-men re-started work.

They forgot any idea of showing the product. Instead they began to show the people who used the toothpaste, in particular an attractive young woman and a handsome young man (suprise, suprise). This couple were photographed in each other's arms, their eyes meeting, their mouths slightly parted, possibly on the point of a kiss (sex makes people read). But the headline altered by only one word: "*Why Signal has a mouthwash in the stripes*". WHY allowed the advertiser to imply benefits to his toothpaste which the picture amplified a hundred times.

Here is another example when WHY adds interest to a headline. We all know many scientists are in favour of banning the bomb. So a headline that said "*Scientists want to ban atom bomb*" is old news. But if you twist the tale a bit, and write "*Why the men who invented the bomb now want to ban it*" – you've improved the interest-rating considerably. Almost as considerably as if you ran a feature titled: "*How to finally ban nuclear weapons*". These alternative headlines promise news, information, unrevealed facts and close reasoning. It can all belong to you if you use the WHY technique.

More examples

Let's say you run a shop, garage or restaurant, and 100,000 customers have passed through your doors. This is good news since it shows you are a popular entrepreneur, who offers excellent service. You could well take an advertisement in your local newspaper, showing the 100,000th customer being welcomed across the threshold with a glass of free champagne. You've seen the kind of thing I mean many times, indeed your local newspaper might give you the publicity free. In a week it's gone, the news-value has passed away, yet it took you many years to clock up all those buyers, So what's to do? Next time you run your advertisement or print your brochure, you show your goods, your prices, your amenities, and all the things that make you special, and you use the word WHY.

Why 100,000 customers have come to Joe's.

That way your story can live a lot longer than just the week when the event took place, and you can show your goods, and sell them hard, rather than show the customer gulping your free champagne. Say you run a firm of solicitors, and you have a client for whom you carried out an especially fine job. Maybe you helped him win a case where he was badly wronged. You talk to your client and he agrees (the matter being suitable) to allow you to feature him in your advertising. You could show a head-and-shoulders picture of your client, with a headline: "*I took my case to Smith, Smith and Smith.*" But that's boring, so instead you show two pictures, one of a terribly crashed car, the other of a brand new car with your client standing proudly beside it, and you have him say:

Why I took my case to Smith, Smith and Smith.

Say you run a local bakery and you're especially good at pastries. And your rival, for all his virtues, can't bake the goodies as well as you. There would be nothing wrong with an advertisement which showed your best pastries, laid out on the page, oozing appetite appeal, with a line inviting customers to buy at Pat's Pastry Shop. But how much more competitive if you get in a little dig at your rival:

Why even other bakers admire Pat's Pastry Shop.

What's more, when you use the HOW TO approach you're stuck with having to add the two words to the beginning of each headline. But when you use WHY, the variations are greater, and you can produce headlines with variety.

Even other bakers admire Pat's Pastry Shop.
And you can see why.

Ten reasons why Pat's Pastry Shop is best.

Pat makes 20 different pastries.
Why so many, and which is best for you?

The town's top hotelier tells why he prefers the pastries from Pat's shop.

I hope these examples, plus others you come across as you look through your newspapers and weekly magazines, give you enough of an idea how these techniques can be used. They have been tried and tested by generations of writers and we know, from research and by comparing the number of replies received from certain advertisements, that HOW and WHY out-pull other approaches. So when you have your headline, or main promise, pause and consider whether it could be improved still further, by hiring Kipling's honest serving men.

The WHEN Technique

This, as you've probably guessed, is to do with time. The times when your product or service is at its most useful. The times when it would be most put to the test. Times when a customer might expect it to fail, but in fact it comes up trumps. Say you're selling a new line in raincoats: you get somebody to pose in your best-looking coat in a thunderstorm, and say: **"It's at times like this you really appreciate my coats"**. Or, if it's sheepskin you're selling, stand your model in a snow-storm. Or welly-boots, and you stand your model in a mud-sodden dirt track. Or washing machines, and you have a line of kids in blackened sports-shirts. You've got the idea, and it can apply to almost any product or service. But it's only one way to exploit the WHEN approach.

Another way is to put what you sell in a torture test situation. We've spoken about torture tests previously, but if you sell stainless-steel wall-ties, for example, and your competition offers only the galvanised version, you show his product rusted and on the point of snapping and *compare it* with your own version, that has stood up to time and the corrosive effects of weather. Again, **"It's at times like this you realise the value of stainless-steel ties"**. Or you've got a new line of suits; show them in important, formal situations, say a man going in for an interview for a new job, with the line: **"The kind of suit that could get you a job"**.

You could promote something by advertising it in the past, say a Christmas pudding, or jam, marmalade, **"My recipe puts the taste of Christmas pudding/jam/marmalade back 60 years"**, or free-range poultry, **"My birds put the taste of chicken back 60 years"**. And you talk about the special way you feed your hens, how they're allowed to roam free, how they're only 16 weeks old when you prepare them for cooking, and so on. Or instead, put the clock forward, and show your fireplaces in the year 2020. The people in your picture are dressed futuristically, but the fireplaces look totally in place, and seem as good as the day they were installed. Your story is that they're designed to stand the test of passing fashions, and built to last. To exploit the WHEN technique in your advertising, ask yourself these questions:

When is my product most needed?
When will it be most appreciated?
When will it be under its fiercest test?
When will it be seen to best advantage?
When will the user get most pleasure from it?
When can it be expected to fail (you prove it won't)?

Sun-tan lotions protect when on the beach or at the swimming-pool, soft drinks are consumed after strenuous exercise, cameras are most used at weddings, vacuum-flasks come into their own at picnics, accountants are important when you start a business, solicitors matter when you buy a house, draw up a will, seek a separation or are about to sign an important contract, fresh lemons are squandered on Shrove Tuesday, sales of flowers blossom on Mother's Day. Decide when your product or service is used the most and see if you can build your advertising round the situation. It takes what could be a plain and simple announcement and adds interest to your story.

The WHERE technique

Now we're dealing with *places*. Major advertisers add style and class to a range of dresses by having them photographed in Venice – that fair city was even used in to entice us to enjoy Cornetto Ice-Cream. Scottish castles sell tartans and whisky, Wimbledon sells tennis racquets, 32-ton trucks sell Yorkie Bars (though for the life of me I can't understand why). Your home-made marmalade would look good on some duke or earl's breakfast table, I don't need to go on because you've got the idea. To exploit the WHERE technique, ask the same questions as for WHEN:

Where is the product most needed?
Where will it look it's best?
Where will it meet it's fiercest test?
Where can it borrow style from?
Where will the user get most pleasure from it?
Where could it be expected to fail (of course it doesn't)?

CHAPTER TWELVE

So far I've cited examples which are obvious and expected, but why not turn the situation upside down? What's wrong with showing bikinis in a snow-scene, fresh strawberries on a shiny stainless-steel table, a luxury mink-coat in Coronation Street, the idea being to create *contrast* and so increase the attention value of your picture. Recently there has been a move to show jewellery on models wearing nothing else – this is not so much to be salacious as to direct the reader to the jewels to the exclusion of everything else. Again I would direct you to study magazines where photographers have been invited to show off the latest in menswear, or vintage cars, or whatever subject the editor thinks will make a good photo-essay. There's nothing wrong in stealing the idea and adapting it for yourself.

The WHO technique

The WHO technique is when you take a well-known personality and make him (or her) the spokesman for your product or service. Well-known sportsmen open shops, well-known film stars show themselves at charity bazaars, authors sign their books, directors flog their films by being interviewed in the press; indeed if you're at all well known there's a good chance that someone will ask you to promote something, sometime, somewhere. But more often than not, with famous people is where most of us think the WHO technique begins and ends. In fact, it isn't so.

Animals and stuffed toys are also part of the WHO game. How often have you seen a bear selling a beer? Or honey-monster selling cereal? And this line stretches to include Muppets, pedigree dogs (who help sell pet-foods), Disney characters which can be tacked to almost anything, and Emu, Basil Brush and Orville who are all waiting in the wings (or until their TV contracts expire).

Humans, animals – after them come all the cartoon characters that ever existed. Superman exhorting us not to smoke cigarettes. The Smurfs, who tried to persuade us to buy a certain petrol. The Rumble-tums, Speedy Alka Seltzer, Winnie the Pooh, Frogs and Princes, all these characters used in advertising (and journalism) belong to the WHO technique.

Finally, there is the ADVERTISER WHO FEATURES HIM-SELF. This is a well-known way of advertising, and provided the individual is appropriate and presentable, for goodness' sake why not? Who doesn't know the marvellous Bernard Matthews, Norfolk Turkey King, whose birds (and their spare parts) are just "bootiful"?

DO YOUR OWN ADVERTISING

How you can use the WHO technique
More likely than not, your budget won't run to featuring a megastar in your advertising. But you can create your own characters, be they animal or human, and have an artist bring them to life in your work. The secret is to ask yourself which characters you can exploit. They can be historic (how often have you seen Henry VIII?) – or fictional – Dracula/Alice/Sherlock Holmes (make sure whoever you use is out of copyright). They can be from the future, or they can be from another planet, and funny with it, like the Smash Martians. Just to give you an idea how silly – yet effective – the game can be, there is a successful cat-food in the USA, named *Miaow*, which was sold by testimonials ostensibly written by (you guessed) cats.

13

HOW TO JUDGE YOUR ADVERTISING.
EIGHT WAYS TO CHECK YOU'VE GOT IT RIGHT.

"When your story is written, go back and cross out the first paragraph."

Advice to journalists

CHAPTER THIRTEEN

We've come to the hard bit, where you the creator have to decide whether what you've written is right, and good enough to appear in print. This is the moment of truth; once you print it's too late to alter, correct or improve. You've got X thousand copies of your brochure in the office and you're stuck with them. If you think it's easy to be objective about advertising you've done yourself, read the story of the role-reversal seminars.

If you've ever used an advertising agent, you'll know that twice a year, in the spring and autumn, the agency invites you to a major presentation, where they show you the work they think you should run for the next six months, tell you why they've done it that way, and what they expect it to achieve. These meetings can be very exciting, for you're shown an advertising campaign which hopefully stimulates, informs and persuades, so you should, to say the least, be stimulated. At the end of the presentation, you, the client, are invited to make your comments, and eventually to approve the advertising. Most of the time, clients who use agents *do* approve the work. But there can always be disagreements, and there's nothing to stop you pulling the advertisements to pieces, and telling your agents to start again. You won't be popular but you are perfectly within your rights, since you know what's best for your business, and you pay the bills. There will be some resistance from the agent, who if he is conscientious will have given a deal of thought to preparing your advertising; however, if your arguments are persuasive enough, you should carry the day. But occasionally the agent gets his own back by inviting you to a role-reversal seminar.

These are three-day events, which take place over a long weekend. The advertising agents hire a university college during vacation time, invite fifty or sixty businessmen along, and give them a chance to experience what it's like on the agent's side of the fence. The businessmen divide into teams. Each has seconded to it a "wrist" – that is a professional artist who will draw anything he's told to, but is not allowed to suggest what should be drawn, since all ideas must come from the customer – you. Each team is given a brief, based on a case-history, and invited to make advertising recommendations which solve the particular marketing problem: in other words they have to get down and produce some advertising, be it for the newspapers or TV, and present it to the seminar jury, who are of course the agents.

The businessmen take these seminars seriously, since not only are they expensive to attend, but they give an opportunity to experience what it's like to start with a product on the one hand, and a blank piece of paper on the other, and know that in a couple of days you've got to present your ideas before the whole workshop, where they will be open to criticism from professional advertising people.

The most frequently heard phrases after these seminars come to a close are: "Gee, I never knew it was so hard". And (music to the agents' ears) "I'll be more understanding with my advertising people in future". And the most amusing aspect of the affair, and the most thought-provoking if you're producing your own advertising, is how often people will stand up and vehemently defend work which is obviously not up to the mark. But they insist it's right *because they've done it*. They've eaten, dreamed, and lived the problem, and when they finally arrive at a solution they cling to it like a drunken sailor to a lamp-post. They haven't put their heart and soul into devising the work to have some idiot tell them it isn't good enough. Don't get me wrong; identification with work is not confined to the non-ad-man. It's just as common inside the advertising business. It has proved so hard to do that the initiators will go to the wall believing their ideas are easy to understand and cannot fail to sell the goods, when in fact those of us not so close can see they might easily be improved. I'd like a pound for every time I've heard a professional issue forth about how apposite his work is, whilst the customer he did it for is thinking exactly the opposite. Now if the full-timers can get too subjective about what they create, how much more easily can it happen to someone experiencing the sweat and toil for the first time?

What remedy against the ego?

Assuming you haven't been to a role-reversal seminar, what can you do to avoid approving second-rate advertising? Naturally it helps to know how easy it is to become identified with; once warned, watch for the traits in yourself. Another good policy is to be your own fiercest critic, never afraid to ask yourself whether there isn't a simpler, quicker way of saying something. Pretend when you've done the final job that you're looking at the first draft. If you really can't trust yourself to be hard on your own brainchild, here are a few rules by which you can judge whether or not advertising is good (and by good, we can only mean effective).

Make space for yourself

You probably remember I suggested that after you had gathered together all the information about the product, the customer and the competition, you gave yourself a breather before you began to write the ad. Well, when you have the finished version of what you think your advertising should be, bend the grey-matter to some new problem, for as long as it takes to erase the agonies of creation. After you've been engrossed in something completely different, come back to your advertising. Creating the distance, far from lending enchantment, lends objectivity. Now, take your advertisement or brochure or whatever, and looking at it *as if for the first time*, ask yourself the following:

1. Is it clear who you're talking to?

I cannot say too often, if you prepare advertising that tries to reach everybody, it'll reach nobody. There are times when you can use your *media* to find your audience with precision. For example, if you have life-jackets to sell, you're half-way there if you advertise in publications like *Yachting News*. But even in *Yachting News* it does no harm if you preface your announcement with a lead-in like: "A major step forward in life-saving equipment for the regular yachtsman".

Advertising researchers tell us that when readers first come to an advertisement, if they see a middle-aged man in it, they assume the piece is meant for middle-aged men, if they see a housewife the ad is for housewives, a pensioner, the story is for pensioners, a baby and it's a baby-product and so on. So those are the two main ways you can be specific about who you're talking to. Either name the kind of person in a small lead-in sub-heading, or show the kind of person in one of your illustrations. Only when you're sure it's plain who you're talking to, go on to the next question.

2. Is it clear what your offer is?

Can you see, without delving into the small print, what offer your advertisement is making? Can you see what is for sale and the reason why the customer should buy it? Never be afraid to seem plain and blunt when it comes to your offer.

There are few advertisers who do this better than Scotcade Ltd; study their three advertisements, for they are clear examples of the discipline. The illustration in each is the product for sale, and you will notice in the case of the Dutch bulbs they don't show the bulbs, but the flowers in bloom, it's not the product that is illustrated, but the promise. This is extolled in the smaller headline at the top of the advertisement: "A dazzling display of colour, that's guaranteed to bloom!" Note the use of the word "guarantee". There is no guarantee

Reproduced by kind permission of Paul Castle, marketing director, Scotcade

in the advertisement, nor a promise of your money back. The main headline is: *500 bulbs for just £14.95*. What could be plainer than that? The chair advertisement offers you the product (illustrated) for £39.95. The alarm clock advertisement (on page 182) shows the product and states the price. Take these advertisements and compare them with your own. Is the offer you make as clear? Good, go on to the next point.

3. Is it interesting?

Interest lies on two levels. The first is where you demonstrate that you are interested in your customers and you do that by talking their language, at their level, without patronising or under-estimating their

Headline promises positive benefit and states price. Specific, not generalised.

Small photograph uses before/after technique.

Sub-headings pick out benefits.

Line illustration adds interest, explains reason why chair helps posture.

Coupon large enough to use easily, contains credit cards.

Illustration of product and how it is used, dominates ad.

Reproduced by kind permission of Paul Castle, marketing director, Scotcade

intelligence. The second level is how interestingly have you *expressed* your offer? You know for yourself, there are some advertisements you never read because they're predictable. Gross offenders are the Building Societies, which bumble on about the best investment and how your money is safe as houses, a pun bad enough to bore a five-year-old. In fact I would say Building Society advertising is, for the most part, dull, exaggerates minimal benefits and assumes we've never seen any before. It talks down to its audience, and can only be described as mundane. Avoid this approach to your work. They use vacuous phrases, show vacuous smiling people, assume the world goes around with its thumb up, and it's a blissful home-owning paradise we snooze in. Since Building Societies aren't profit-making organis-

181

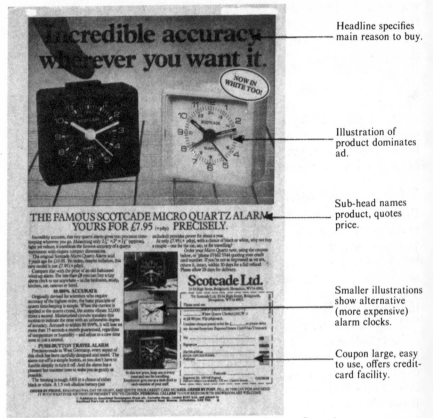

Headline specifies main reason to buy.

Illustration of product dominates ad.

Sub-head names product, quotes price.

Smaller illustrations show alternative (more expensive) alarm clocks.

Coupon large, easy to use, offers credit-card facility.

Reproduced by kind permission of Paul Castle, marketing director, Scotcade

ations it doesn't matter if their work is seen or not. Please see that your advertisements are never as bland.

4. Is your advertisement instant?

I'm talking about how fast it communicates. If you take a look at your morning paper, you see there are two kinds of advertisements. The first is where you look at the picture, read the headline and with a frisson of comprehension running down your spine, glide painlessly into the small print. This kind of advertisement is rare, generally occupies a big space in your paper (a half or a whole page) and has probably been prepared by a top agency. The second kind is where you look at the picture, read the headline and you're no further forward with the story than a vague feeling that there's nothing to interest you here. This second kind of advertisement is so common it is only surprising that the people who pay for them don't protest to the people who create them, about how slow they are in getting to their point. And that is what I mean by your advertisement being *instant*.

The trick is to try and create what I call a telegram – get over nearly all your story with a picture and a headline. Many advertisers have to do that when they create a poster. Posters are instant and high-speed messages win you hard cash.

5. Is your advertisement believable?

Belief exists on two levels. First is the belief that the promise you make is true. Second the belief in the *way* you make it. Let me give you an example where the promise made about the product is beyond belief. Birds, the custard people, introduced into the instant coffee market a new, mellow blend to rival Nescafé and Maxwell House. Their advertising people came up with a TV commercial of women looking grim at "ordinary" coffee while a choir twittered the line *"Mellow Birds will make you smile"*.

Now coffee can stimulate you; induce you to ask for a second cup; make you compliment the hostess; remind you of that most famous of all coffees, from the blue mountains of Jamaica; bathe your tongue in volatiles and delight your nose. There are probably a dozen things it can do for you, but sure as eggs, no coffee on earth ever made me smile. So what happened? Well, the people who wrote the commercial fell into their office, closed the door, and disappeared down a tunnel into Ad-Land. Ad-Land is the place where everything is new, better, more exciting. Mention the product and eyes roll. Suggest benefits and heavenly choirs sing. In Ad-Land people believe anything about the product, however banal and unlikely it may be, and there is absolutely no connection with this crazy place and the world where products are seen, tasted, compared and paid for in cash. Ad-Land is bad-land; don't go there, for when you return with your advertisement it will be seen for the foolish, unbelievable thing it is.

That is the first level of believability. Next, check if you've made your promise in the most believable way. David Ogilvy, guru of the advertising industry, has a foolproof method of testing that. He says (and I paraphrase), "If you are willing to say to your wife the things you write in your advertisement, if you are convinced that she will accept those things, and not sneer or snigger at them, then your advertisement is believable." Wow, the acid test. Will the missus fall for this?

And here are some things *not* to do. Do not, when you look at your work, argue that although you do not believe it, people who are less intelligent or less well-informed will. Do not pretend anyone ignorant of the product will believe it. And do not think because it will shortly appear in print, backed by a large and attractive photograph, it will seem believable. Yes, printed material does carry an authority of its own, but you are facing an audience of hard-nosed customers, not willing to part with their hard-earned cash. They are no more gullible than the rest of us. Stand back from your work, read it through and say: Do I believe this? Would my wife (or husband) who knows me better than anyone, believe? If you can say "Yes", go to the next point.

6. Is it the right length?

How long should an advertisement be?

> *Short enough to be read to the end.*
> *Long enough to make the sale.*

There are no rules. Some people will tell you that on certain products, it's good policy to deliberately over-write. That way, they argue, people will believe there's a lot to be said for the product. "But," I said to a man who put forward this argument, "if the advertisement is over-written nobody will read it." "No matter," was his reply, "provided they think the product has much to commend it."

Well, it's a point of view and not one I'll buy, thank you. Your advertisement should say enough to answer the reader's quest for information. It should go on to persuade him to act, then call it a day. Advertisers on TV with half-minute commercials (which are far and away the kind that most often appear) get their story across in sixty words – that's two words per second, the speed a good announcer speaks. You'll use newspaper advertising and can say a lot more, and the reader has time to read a lot more. If you use a direct sales-letter, then you can reiterate your promises several different ways, and the repetition can pay dividends. In the end, it's a matter of common sense. If you make sound promises, and coax the reader from one sentence to the next, you'll hold attention – just so long as you say something new. When there's nothing left unsaid, and you start to repeat yourself – stop.

7. Is it clear what the customer has to do?

What can you hope the average reader will do at the end of the average advertisement?

(a) Complete a coupon.

(b) Make a 'phone call.

(c) Fill in an order form and write a cheque.

(d) Write a letter (to their MP, local councillor, 10 Downing Street).

(e) Give money to charity.

(f) Become a member of a club/organisation (AA, RAC, Diner's Club).

(g) Apply for a catalogue.

(h) Change their mind, and believe something they didn't believe before.

(i) Begin to develop an attitude.

(j) Get angry. (About nuclear missiles, killing whales).

(k) Be in the right frame of mind when your rep calls.

The point about the above is to get you to remember to *tell your customer what you want him to do*. Come right out and issue instructions (in the nicest possible way). You haven't spent money in the hope of reinforcing apathy. You want action – ask for it by name.

8. Have you proved your case?

When a major advertiser makes a claim, it's very often difficult – if not impossible – to prove. Take, for example, the Lyons/Tetley breakfast cereal Ready-Brek. For years they've been running TV commercials which claim that Ready-Brek is "Central Heating for Kids". We know what they mean, but it's an impossible thing to prove. The way they get us to accept the idea is to keep saying it, not just for a winter, not just for three or four years, but for a decade and a half. They understand that "repetition is reputation", and they are competing against Kelloggs, who do exactly the same thing, and tell us cornflakes are the "Sunshine Breakfast".

The smaller advertiser, on the other hand, can very often prove his claims, or at least present them, in a way that makes them convincing. I have stressed the importance of using facts in your advertising, and seeking out specifics to substantiate promises. When deciding if your work passes all the tests in this chapter, here's one final checklist:

(a) Photographs prove what your product looks like. Use them instead of drawings.

(b) Use case-histories of satisfied customers.

(c) Use direct quotations from buyers.

(d) Use any support from a professional body: the BS Kitemark, the Design Council Award, the Royal Warrant.

(e) Use a guarantee.

(f) Use quotations from magazines that have tested your product.

(g) Use comparison charts that line up what you offer against the competition.

(h) Use a list of your existing clients, especially if it includes well-known names.

(i) Offer a trial sample in your coupon.

And remember the truth about what you're selling – the properly researched truth – is *always* better than anything you can dream up.

What if – after all this – you turn your own work down?

You're either an impossible perfectionist, or you've decided that DIY advertising is not for you. Then you have to pick someone to write your advertising for you, and if that is your chosen course, here are some last points to help you.

Remember, your writer is the person who articulates your promises and presents the case for your company. There's no one more important in the business of advertising. To find a good writer, ask around your business colleagues to see who they can recommend. If nothing comes of this, turn to *Yellow Pages*, or *The Creative Handbook*. Either way you'll be choosing blind, but *The Creative Handbook* gives you a much wider choice. Their address is Reed Information Services,

CHAPTER THIRTEEN

Windsor Court, East Grinstead House, East Grinstead, West Sussex RH19 1XA. Telephone 0342-326972. The Handbook lists Advertising Consultants, Designers, Copywriters, Illustrators, Cartoonists, Photographers and Photographic Libraries, area by area, so you will be able to see who's nearest to you, and get them to come and see you.

Always see two or three copywriters, and ask them to bring samples of their work. Listen to them talk about why they've done the jobs the way they have. Probe to see if they know their subjects *in depth*. If a writer has a lot of work for one firm – or a couple of firms – then at least you can be sure he's doing a good job for them. Don't be surprised if some writers don't have reams of work to show: sometimes it's difficult to get samples of the material after it's been printed. But be wary of those with no samples – or very few. They're not trying.

You can ask whether the writer has an artist he works with. If so, that will save you having to find your own designers. If you decide to give him the job, then you must be sure he has access to the kind of information I've described throughout this book. Give him time to do his homework. Give him the most thorough briefing you can, telling him who you want to reach and what you want to say.

Be punctilious about money. Agree a fee up-front, before work is started. Be sure you know what you're getting for your money. The words only, or words and a rough scamp of how they're intended to look, or words and a finished visualisation of the brochure or advertisement, rendered by an artist. And make sure when you negotiate the fee that you've made provision for corrections and alterations. If the writer has to go back and start again, what is the financial position on the work he's done already?

When you've found someone you like, involve him as closely with your aims as you can. A comprehensive brief, that includes details of your product, your competitors' products, your market, the media you want to use, the budget, your objectives and all the product benefits, will repay the time spent on it manyfold. The biggest harm you can do to yourself is to ask your copywriter to produce "bricks" without giving him enough straw.

In conclusion, I would commend to you the advice about advertising which comes quite free of charge from your Post Office Postal Sales Representative. Although he's officially interested only in direct-mail selling, where you use his postal services, you can, in fact, ask him a good deal about how to begin an advertising programme, provided it's clear that, at the end of the day, there will be something in it for him.

DO YOUR OWN ADVERTISING

The disciplines and guidelines in this book are a synopsis of three decades of creative experience, working with some of the most successful advertising agents in Britain, for some of the best-known business names. The boast of the professional copywriter is that he can sell you anything: I'd like to wish you good luck in writing your advertising, whatever you have to sell.

INDEX